D0983676

HOW FICTION WORKS

HOW FICTION WORKS

James Wood

JONATHAN CAPE
LONDON

Published by Jonathan Cape 2008

2 4 6 8 10 9 7 5 3 1

Copyright © James Wood 2008

James Wood has asserted his right under the Copyright, Designs
and Patents Act 1988 to be identified as the author of this work

First published in Great Britain in 2008 by
Jonathan Cape
Random House, 20 Vauxhall Bridge Road, London SW1V 2SA

www.rbooks.co.uk

Addresses for companies within The Random House Group Limited
can be found at: www.randomhouse.co.uk/offices.htm

The Random House Group Limited Reg. No. 954009

A CIP catalogue record for this book is available from the British Library

ISBN 9780224079839 (Hardback edition)
ISBN 9780224079846 (Trade paperback edition)

The Random House Group Limited makes every effort to ensure that the papers
used in its books are made from trees that have been legally sourced from well-
managed and credibly certified forests. Our paper procurement policy can be
found at www.rbooks.co.uk/environment

Typeset in Adobe Garamond by Palimpsest Book Production Limited
Grangemouth, Stirlingshire
Printed and bound in Great Britain by
CPI Mackays, Chatham ME5 8TD

for Norman and Elsa Rush
and for C. D. M.

'There is only one recipe – to care a great deal
for the cookery.'

Henry James

CONTENTS

INTRODUCTION

In 1857, John Ruskin wrote a little book called *The Elements of Drawing*. It is a patient primer, intended, by casting a critic's eye over the business of creation, to help the practising painter, the curious viewer, the ordinary art-lover. Ruskin begins by urging his readers to look at nature – to look, say, at a leaf, and then to copy it in pencil. He includes his own drawing of a leaf. He moves from a leaf to a painting by Tintoretto: notice the brushstrokes, says Ruskin, see how he draws the hands, look at how he pays attention to the shading. Step by step, Ruskin takes his readers through the processes of creation. His authority comes not from his own technique as a draughtsman – he was an accomplished artist but not a greatly gifted one – but from what his eye has seen, and how well, and his ability to transmit that vision into prose.

There are surprisingly few books like this about fiction. E. M. Forster's *Aspects of the Novel*, published in 1927, is canonical for good reason, but now seems imprecise. I admire Milan Kundera's three books on the art of fiction, but Kundera is a novelist and essayist rather than a practical critic; occasionally we want his hands to be a bit inkier with text.

My two favourite twentieth-century critics of the novel are the Russian formalist Viktor Shklovsky, and the French formalist-cum-structuralist Roland Barthes. Both were great critics because, being formalists, they thought like writers: they attended to style, to words, to form, to metaphor and imagery. But Barthes and Shklovsky thought like writers alienated from creative instinct, and were drawn, like larcenous bankers, to raid again and again the very source that sustained them – literary style. Perhaps because of this alienation, this aggressive passion, they come to conclusions about the novel that seem to me interesting but wrong-headed, and this book conducts a sustained argument with them.

And both are specialists, writing, in the end, for other specialists; Barthes in particular, does not write as if he expects to be read and comprehended by any kind of common reader (even one who is in training for uncommonness . . .)

In this book I try to ask some of the essential questions about the art of fiction. Is realism real? How do we define a successful metaphor? What is a character? When do we recognise a brilliant use of detail in fiction? What is point of view, and how does it work? What is imaginative sympathy? Why does fiction move us? These are old questions, some of which have been resuscitated by recent work in academic criticism and literary theory; but I am not sure that academic criticism and literary theory have answered them very well. I hope, then, that this book might be one which asks theoretical questions but answers them practically – or to say it differently, asks a critic's questions and offers a writer's answers.

If the book has a larger argument, it is that fiction is both artifice and verisimilitude, and that there is nothing difficult in holding together these two possibilities. That is why I have tried to give the most detailed accounts of the technique of that artifice – of how fiction works – in order to reconnect that technique to the world, as Ruskin wanted to connect Tintoretto's work to how we look at a leaf. As a result, the chapters of this book have a way of collapsing into each other, because each is motivated by the same aesthetic: when I talk about free indirect style I am really talking about point of view, and when I am talking about point of view I am really talking about the perception of detail, and when I am talking about detail I am really talking about character, and when I am talking about character I am really talking about *the real*, which is at the bottom of my enquiries.

A NOTE ON FOOTNOTES
AND DATES

Mindful of the common reader, I have tried to reduce what Joyce calls 'the true scholastic stink' to bearable levels. Footnotes draw attention only to obscure or otherwise hard-to-find sources; in them, I give the date of first publication but not the location or publisher (these facts being nowadays much more easily attainable than they used to be). In the text itself, I have suppressed most of the publication dates of the novels and stories I discuss; in a bibliography, I list all those novels and stories in chronological order, with dates of first publication provided.

As a teenager I was very taken by the rather fancy note to Ford Madox Ford's *The English Novel*: 'This book was written in New York, on board the S.S. *Patria*, and in the port and neighbourhood of Marseilles during July and August, 1927.' I cannot claim any proximate glamour, nor a similar feat of library-less memory, but in the spirit of Ford, I can say that I have used only the books I actually own – the books at hand in my study – to produce this little book. I can also add that, except for a paragraph here and there, none of this book has been previously published.

NARRATING

1

The house of fiction has many windows, but only two or three doors. I can tell a story in the third person or in the first person, and perhaps in the second person singular or in the first person plural, though successful examples of these latter two are rare indeed. And that is it. Anything else probably will not much resemble narration; it may be closer to poetry, or prose-poetry.

2

In reality, we are stuck with third- and first-person narration. The common idea is that there is a contrast between reliable narration (third person omniscience) and unreliable narration (the unreliable first-person narrator, who knows less about himself than the reader eventually does). On one side, Tolstoy, say; and on the other, Humbert Humbert or Italo Svevo's narrator, Zeno Cosini, or Bertie Wooster. Authorial omniscience, people assume, has had its day, much as that 'vast moth-eaten musical brocade called religion' has also had its. W. G. Sebald once said to me, 'I think that fiction writing which does not acknowledge the uncertainty of the narrator himself, is a form of imposture which I find very, very difficult to take. Any form of authorial writing where the narrator sets himself up as stagehand and director and judge and executor in a text, I find somehow unacceptable. I cannot bear to read books of this kind.' Sebald continued: 'If you refer to Jane Austen, you refer to a world where there were set standards of propriety which were accepted by everyone. Given that you have a world where the rules are clear and where one knows where trespassing begins, then I think it is legitimate, within that context, to be a narrator who knows what the rules are and who knows the answers to certain questions. But I think these certainties have been taken from us by the course of history, and that we do have to acknowledge our own sense of ignorance and of insufficiency in these matters and therefore to try and write accordingly.'[1]

3

For Sebald, and for many writers like him, standard third-person omniscient narration is a kind of antique cheat. But both sides of this division have been caricatured.

4

Actually, first-person narration is generally more reliable than unreliable; and third person 'omniscient' narration is generally more partial than omniscient.

---

[1] This interview can be found in *Brick* magazine, volume 10. Sebald's German accent had a way of exaggerating the already comic, miserable, Bernhard-like pleasure he took in stressing words like 'very' and 'unacceptable'.

The first-person narrator is often highly reliable; Jane Eyre, a highly reliable first-person narrator, for instance, tells us her story from a position of belated enlightenment (years later, married to Mr Rochester, she can now see her whole life-story, rather as Mr Rochester's eyesight is gradually returning at the end of the novel). Even the apparently unreliable narrator is more often than not reliably unreliable. Think of Kazuo Ishiguro's butler in *The Remains of the Day*, or of Bertie Wooster, or even of Humbert Humbert. We know that the narrator is being unreliable because the author is alerting us, through reliable manipulation, to that narrator's unreliability. A process of authorial flagging is going on; the novel teaches us how to read its narrator.

Unreliably unreliable narration is very rare, actually – about as rare as a genuinely mysterious, truly bottomless character. The nameless narrator of Knut Hamsun's *Hunger* is highly unreliable, and finally unknowable (it helps that he is insane); Dostoevsky's underground narrator, in *Notes from Underground*, is the model for Hamsun. Italo Svevo's Zeno Cosini may be the best example of truly unreliable narration. He imagines that by telling us his life-story he is psychoanalysing himself (he has promised his analyst to do this). But his self-comprehension, waved confidently before our eyes, is as comically perforated as a bullet-holed flag.

5

On the other side, omniscient narration is rarely as omniscient as it seems. To begin with, authorial style generally has a way of making third-person omniscience seem partial and inflected. Authorial style tends to draw our attention towards the writer,

7

towards the artifice of the author's construction, and so towards the writer's own impress. Thus the almost comic paradox of Flaubert's celebrated wish that the author be 'impersonal', God-like, removed, and the high personality of his very style, those exquisite sentences and details, which are nothing less than God's showy signatures on every page: so much for the impersonal author. Tolstoy comes closest to a canonical idea of authorial omniscience, and he uses with great naturalness and authority a mode of writing that Roland Barthes called 'the reference code' (or sometimes 'the cultural code'), whereby a writer makes confident appeal to a universal or consensual truth, or a body of shared cultural or scientific knowledge.[2]

6

So-called omniscience is almost impossible. As soon as someone tells a story about a character, narrative seems to want to bend itself around that character, wants to merge with that character, to take on his or her way of thinking and speaking. A novelist's omniscience soon enough becomes a kind of secret sharing; this is called *free indirect style*, a term

---

[2] Barthes uses this term in his book *S/Z* (1970; trans. Richard Miller, 1974). He means the way that nineteenth-century writers refer to commonly accepted cultural or scientific knowledge, for instance shared ideological generalities about 'women'. I extend the term to cover any kind of authorial generalisation. For instance, an example from Tolstoy: at the start of *The Death of Ivan Ilyich*, three of Ivan Ilyich's friends are reading his obituary, and Tolstoy writes that each man, 'as is usual in such cases, was secretly congratulating himself that it was Ivan who had died and not him'. *As is usual in such cases*: the author refers with ease and wisdom to a central human truth, serenely gazing into the hearts of three different men.

novelists have lots of different nicknames for – 'close third person', or 'going into character'.[3]

7

a) 'He looked over at his wife. "She looks so unhappy," he thought, "almost sick." He wondered what to say.' – This is direct or quoted speech ('"She looks so unhappy," he thought to himself') combined with the character's reported or indirect speech ('He wondered what to say.') The old-fashioned notion of a character's thought as a speech made to himself, a kind of internal address.

b) 'He looked over at his wife. She looked so unhappy, he thought, almost sick. He wondered what to say.' – This is reported or indirect speech, the internal speech of the husband reported by the author, and flagged as such ('he thought'). It is the most recognisable, the most habitual of all the codes of standard realist narrative.

c) 'He looked at his wife. Yes, she was tiresomely unhappy again, almost sick. What the hell should he say?' – This is free indirect speech or style: the husband's internal speech or thought has been freed of its authorial flagging; no 'he said to himself' or 'he wondered' or 'he thought'.

Note the gain in flexibility. The narrative seems to float away from the novelist and take on the properties of the character, who now seems to 'own' the words. The writer is free to inflect the reported thought, to bend it round the character's own words ('What the hell should he say?'). We

---

[3] I like D. A. Miller's phrase for free indirect style, from his book *Jane Austen, or the Secret of Style* (2003): 'close writing'.

are close to stream of consciousness, and that is the direction free indirect style takes in the nineteenth and early twentieth centuries: 'He looked at her. Unhappy, yes. Sickly. Obviously a big mistake to have told her. His stupid conscience again. Why did he blurt it? All his own fault, and what now?'

You will note that such internal monologue, freed from flagging and quotation marks, sounds very much like the pure soliloquy of eighteenth- and nineteenth-century novels (an example of a technical improvement merely renovating, in a circular manner, an original technique too basic and useful – too real – to do without).

8

Free indirect style is at its most powerful when hardly visible or audible: 'Ted watched the orchestra through stupid tears.' In my example, the word 'stupid' marks the sentence as written in free indirect style. Remove it, and we have standard reported thought: 'Ted watched the orchestra through tears.' The addition of the word 'stupid' raises the question: whose word is this? It's unlikely that I would want to call my character stupid merely for listening to some music in a concert hall. No, in a marvellous alchemical transfer, the word now belongs partly to Ted. He is listening to the music and crying, and is embarrassed – we can imagine him furiously rubbing his eyes – that he has allowed these 'stupid' tears to fall. Convert it back into first-person speech, and we have this: '"Stupid to be crying at this silly piece of Brahms," he thought.' But this example is several words longer; and we have lost the complicated presence of the author.

What is so useful about free indirect style is that in our example a word like 'stupid' somehow belongs both to the author and the character; we are not entirely sure who 'owns' the word. Might 'stupid' reflect a slight asperity or distance on the part of the author? Or does the word belong *wholly* to the character, with the author, in a rush of sympathy, having 'handed' it, as it were, to the tearful fellow?

Thanks to free indirect style, we see things through the character's eyes and language but also through the author's eyes and language, too. We inhabit omniscience and partiality at once. A gap opens between author and character, and the bridge – which is free indirect style itself – between them simultaneously closes that gap and draws attention to its distance.

This is merely another definition of dramatic irony: to see through a character's eyes while being encouraged to see more than the character can see (an unreliability identical to the unreliable first-person narrator's).

Some of the purest examples of this dramatic irony are found in children's literature, which often needs to allow a child – or the child's proxy, an animal – to see the world through limited eyes, while alerting the older reader to this limitation. In Robert McCloskey's *Make Way for Ducklings*, Mr and Mrs Mallard are trying out the Boston Public Gardens for their new home, when a Swan boat (a boat made to look like a swan but actually powered by a pedal-pushing human pilot) passes them. Mr Mallard has never seen anything like this before. McCloskey falls naturally into free indirect style: 'Just as they were getting ready to start on their way, a strange enormous bird came by. It was pushing a boat full of people, and there was a man sitting on its back. "Good morning," quacked Mr Mallard, being polite. The big bird was too proud to answer.' Instead of telling us that Mr Mallard could make no sense of the swan boat, McCloskey places us in Mr Mallard's confusion; yet the confusion is obvious enough that a broad ironic gap opens between Mr Mallard and the reader (or author). We are not confused in the same way as Mr Mallard; but we are also being made to inhabit Mr Mallard's confusion.

12

What happens, though, when a more serious writer wants to open a very small gap between character and author? What happens when a novelist wants us to inhabit a character's confusion, but will not 'correct' that confusion, refuses to make clear what a state of non-confusion would look like? We can walk in a straight line from McCloskey to Henry James. There is a technical connection, for instance, between *Make Way for Ducklings* and James's novel *What Maisie Knew*. Free indirect style helps us to inhabit juvenile confusion, this time a young girl's rather than a duck's. James tells the story, from the third person, of Maisie Farange, a little girl whose parents have viciously divorced. She is bounced between them, as new governesses, from each parental side, are thrust upon her. James wants us to live inside her confusion, and also wants to describe adult corruption from the eyes of childish innocence. Maisie likes one of her governesses, the plain and distinctly lower-middle-class Mrs Wix, who wears her hair rather grotesquely, and who once had a little daughter called Clara Matilda, a girl who, at around Maisie's age, was knocked down on the Harrow Road, and is buried in the cemetery at Kensal Green. Maisie knows that her elegant and vapid mother does not think much of Mrs Wix, but Maisie likes her all the same:

> It was on account of these things that mamma got her for such low pay, really for nothing: so much, one day when Mrs Wix had accompanied her into the drawing-room and left her, the child heard one of the ladies she found there – a lady with eyebrows arched like skipping-ropes and thick black stitching, like ruled lines for musical notes on beautiful white gloves – announce to another. She knew governesses were poor; Miss Overmore was unmentionably and Mrs Wix ever so publicly so. Neither this, however, nor the old brown frock nor the diadem nor the button, made a difference for Maisie in the charm put forth through everything, the charm of Mrs Wix's conveying that somehow, in her ugliness and her poverty, she was peculiarly and soothingly safe; safer than any one in the world, than papa, than mamma, than the lady with the arched eyebrows; safer even, though so much less beautiful, than Miss Overmore, on whose loveliness, as she supposed it, the little girl was faintly conscious that one couldn't rest with quite the same tucked-in and kissed-for-good-night feeling. Mrs Wix was as safe as Clara

Matilda, who was in heaven and yet, embarrassingly, also in Kensal Green, where they had been together to see her little huddled grave.

What a piece of writing this is! So flexible, so capable of inhabiting different levels of comprehension and irony, so full of poignant identification with young Maisie, yet constantly moving in towards Maisie and moving away from her, back towards the author.

13

James's free indirect style allows us to inhabit at least three different perspectives at once: the official parental and adult judgement on Mrs Wix; Maisie's version of the official view; and Maisie's view of Mrs Wix. The official view, overheard by Maisie, is filtered through Maisie's own half-comprehending voice: 'It was on account of these things that mamma got her for such low pay, really for nothing.' The lady with the arched eyebrows who uttered this cruelty is being paraphrased by Maisie, and paraphrased not especially sceptically or rebelliously, but with a child's wide-eyed respect for authority. James must make us feel that Maisie knows a lot but not enough. Maisie may not like the woman with the arched eyebrows who spoke thus about Mrs Wix, but she is still in fear of her judgement, and we can hear a kind of excited respect in the narration; the free indirect style is done so well that it is *pure voice* – it longs to be turned back into the speech of which it is the paraphrase: we can hear, as a kind of shadow, Maisie saying to the kind of friend she in fact painfully lacks, 'You know, Mamma got her for very low pay because she is very poor and has a dead daughter. I've visited the grave, don't you know!'

So there is the official adult opinion of Mrs Wix; and there is Maisie's comprehension of this official disapproval; and then, countervailingly, there is Maisie's own, much warmer opinion of Mrs Wix, who may not be as elegant as her predecessor, Miss Overmore, but who seems much more safe: the purveyor of a uniquely 'tucked-in and kissed-for-good-night feeling'. (Notice that in the interest of letting Maisie 'speak' through his language, James is willing to sacrifice his own stylistic elegance in a phrase like this.)

14

James's genius gathers in one word: 'embarrassingly'. That is where all the stress comes to rest. 'Mrs Wix was as safe as Clara Matilda, who was in heaven and yet, *embarrassingly*, also in Kensal Green, where they had been together to see her little huddled grave.' Whose word is 'embarrassingly'? It is Maisie's: it is embarrassing for a child to witness adult grief, and we know that Mrs Wix has taken to referring to Clara Matilda as Maisie's 'little dead sister'. We can imagine Maisie standing next to Mrs Wix in the cemetery at Kensal Green – it is characteristic of James's narration that he has not mentioned the place name Kensal Green until now, leaving it for us to work out – we can imagine her standing next to Mrs Wix and feeling awkward and embarrassed, at once impressed and a little afraid of Mrs Wix's grief. And here is the greatness of the passage: Maisie, despite her greater love for Mrs Wix, stands in the same relation to Mrs Wix as she stands to the lady with the arched eyebrows; both women cause her some embarrassment. She fully understands neither, even if she uncomprehendingly prefers the former. 'Embarrassingly': the word encodes Maisie's natural embarrassment and also the internalised embarrassment of official adult opinion ('my dear, it is so *embarrassing*, that woman is always taking her up to Kensal Green!')

15

Remove the word 'embarrassingly' from the sentence and it would barely be free indirect style: 'Mrs Wix was as safe as Clara Matilda, who was in heaven and yet also in Kensal Green, where they had been together to see her little huddled grave.' The addition of the single adverb takes us deep into Maisie's confusion, and at that moment we become her – that adverb is passed from James to Maisie, is given to Maisie. We merge with her. Yet, within the same sentence, having briefly merged, we are drawn back: 'her little *huddled* grave.' 'Embarrassingly' is the word Maisie might have used, but 'huddled' is not. It is Henry James's word. The sentence pulsates, moves in and out, towards the character and away from her – when we reach 'huddled' we are reminded that an *author* allowed us to merge with his character, that the author's magniloquent style is the envelope within which this generous contract is carried.

16

The critic Hugh Kenner writes about a moment in *A Portrait of the Artist as a Young Man* when Uncle Charles 'repairs' to the outhouse. 'Repairs' is a pompous verb which belongs to outmoded poetic convention. It is 'bad' writing. Joyce, with his acute eye for cliché, would only use such a word knowingly. It must be, says Kenner, Uncle Charles's word, the word he might use about himself in his fond fantasy about his own importance ('and so I *repair* to the outhouse'). Kenner names this the Uncle Charles Principle. Mystifyingly, he calls this 'something new in fiction'. Yet we know it isn't. The Uncle Charles principle is just an edition of free indirect style. Joyce is a master at it. 'The Dead' begins like this: 'Lily, the caretaker's daughter, was literally run off her feet.' But no one is *literally* run off her feet. What we hear is Lily saying to herself or to a friend (with great emphasis on precisely the most inaccurate word, and with a strong accent): 'Oi was *lit-er-rully* ron off me feet!'

17

Even if Kenner's example is a bit different, it is still not new. Mock-heroic poetry of the eighteenth century gets its laughs by applying the language of epic or the Bible to reduced human subjects. In Pope's *The Rape of the Lock*, Belinda's make-up and dressing-table effects are seen as 'unnumbered treasures', 'India's glowing gems', 'all Arabia breathes from yonder box', and so on. Part of the joke is that this is the kind of language that the personage – 'personage' being precisely a mock-heroic word – might want to use about herself; the rest of the joke resides in the actual littleness of that personage. Well what is this but an early example of free indirect style?

In the opening of Chapter Five of *Pride and Prejudice*, Jane Austen introduces us to Sir William Lucas, once the mayor of Longbourn, who, knighted by the King, has decided that he is too big for the town, and must move to a new pile:

> Sir William Lucas had been formerly in trade in Meryton, where he had made a tolerable fortune and risen to the honour of knighthood by an address to the King, during his mayoralty. The distinction had perhaps been felt too strongly. It had given him a disgust to his business and to his residence in a small market town; and quitting them both, he had removed with his family to a house about a mile from Meryton, denominated from that period Lucas Lodge, where he could think with pleasure of his own importance . . .

Austen's irony dances over this like the long-legged fly in Yeats's poem: 'where he had made a tolerable fortune'. What is, or would be, a 'tolerable' fortune? Intolerable to whom, tolerated by whom? But the great example of mock-heroic comedy resides in that phrase 'denominated from that period Lucas Lodge'. Lucas Lodge is funny enough; it is like Toad of Toad Hall or Shandy Hall, and we can be sure that the house does not quite measure up to its alliterative grandeur. But the pomposity of 'denominated from that period' is funny because we can imagine Sir William saying to himself 'and I will *denominate* the house, from *this period*, Lucas Lodge. Yes, that sounds *prodigious*.' Mock-heroic is almost identical, at this point, to free indirect style. Austen has handed the language over to Sir William; but she is still tartly in control.

A modern master of the mock-heroic is V. S. Naipaul in *A House for Mr Biswas*: 'When he got home he mixed and drank some MacLean's Brand Stomach Powder, undressed, got into bed, and began to read Epictetus.' The comic-pathetic

capitalisation of the brand name, and the presence of Epictetus
– Pope himself would not have done it better. And what is
the make of the bed that poor Mr Biswas rests on? It is,
Naipaul deliberately tells us every so often, a 'Slumberking
bed': the right name for a man who may be a king or little
god in his own mind but who will never rise above 'Mr'. And
Naipaul's decision, of course, to refer to Biswas as 'Mr Biswas'
throughout the novel has itself a mock-heroic irony about it,
'Mr' being at once the most ordinary honorific and, in a poor
society, a by no means spontaneous achievement. 'Mr Biswas,'
we might say, is free indirect style in a pod: 'Mr' is how Biswas
likes to think of himself; but it is all he will ever be, along
with everyone else.

18

There is a final refinement of free indirect style – we should
now just call it authorial irony – when the gap between
an author's voice and a character's voice seems to collapse
altogether; when a character's voice does indeed seem rebelliously to have taken over the narration altogether. 'The town
was small, worse than a village, and in it lived almost none
but old people, who died so rarely it was even annoying.'
What an amazing opening! It is the first sentence of
Chekhov's story 'Rothschild's Fiddle'. The next sentences are:
'And in the hospital and jail there was very little demand for
coffins. In short, business was bad.' The rest of the paragraph introduces us to an extremely mean coffin-maker, and
we realise that the story has opened in the middle of free
indirect style: 'and in it lived almost none but old people,
who died so rarely it was even annoying.' We are in the

midst of the coffin-maker's mind, for whom longevity is an economic nuisance. Chekhov subverts the expected neutrality of the opening of a story or novel, which might have traditionally begun with a panning shot before we narrow our focus ('The little town of N. was smaller than a village, and had two rather grubby little streets,' etc.). But where Joyce, in 'The Dead', clearly pegs his free indirect style to Lily, Chekhov begins his use of it *before* his character has even been identified. And while Joyce abandons Lily's perspective, moving first into authorial omniscience and then to Gabriel Conroy's point of view, Chekhov's story continues to narrate events from the coffin-maker's eyes.

Or perhaps it might be more accurate to say that the story is written from a point of view closer to a village chorus than to one man. This village chorus sees life pretty much as brutally as the coffin-maker would – 'There were not many patients, and he did not have to wait long, only about three hours' – but continues to see this world after the coffin-maker has died. The Sicilian writer Giovanni Verga (almost exactly contemporaneous with Chekhov) used this kind of village-chorus narration much more systematically than his Russian counterpart. His stories, though written technically in authorial third person, seem to emanate from a community of Sicilian peasants; they are thick with proverbial sayings, truisms, and homely similes.

We can call this 'unidentified free indirect style'.

19

As a logical development of free indirect style, it is not surprising that Dickens, Hardy, Verga, Chekhov, Faulkner, Pavese, Henry

Green and others tend to produce the kinds of similes and metaphors which, while successful and literary enough in their own right, are also the kinds of similes and metaphors that their own characters might produce. When Robert Browning describes the sound of a bird singing its song twice over, in order to 'recapture/ The first fine careless rapture', he is being a poet, trying to find the best poetic image; but when Chekhov, in his story 'Peasants', says that a bird's cry sounded as if a cow had been locked up in a shed all night, he is being a fiction writer: he is thinking like one of his peasants.

20

Seen in this light, there is almost no area of narration not touched by the long finger of free indirect narration – which is to say, by irony. Consider the penultimate chapter of Nabokov's *Pnin*: the comic Russian professor has just given a party, and has received the news that the college where he teaches no longer wants his services. He is sadly washing his dishes, and a nutcracker slips out of his soapy hand and falls into the water, apparently about to break a beautiful submerged bowl. Nabokov writes that the nutcracker falls from Pnin's hands like a man falling from a roof; Pnin tries to grasp it, but 'the leggy thing' slips into the water. 'Leggy thing' is a terrific metaphorical likeness: we can instantly see the long legs of the wayward nutcracker, as if it were falling off the roof and walking away. But 'thing' is even better, *precisely because it is vague*: Pnin is lunging at the implement, and what word in English better conveys a messy lunge, a swipe at verbal meaning, than 'thing'? Now if the brilliant 'leggy' is Nabokov's word, then the hapless 'thing' is Pnin's word, and Nabokov is here using a kind of free indirect style, probably without even thinking about it. As usual, if we turn it into first-person speech, we can hear the way in which the word 'thing' belongs to Pnin and wants to be spoken: 'Come here, you, you . . . oh . . . you annoying *thing*!' Splash.[4]

21

It is useful to watch good writers make mistakes. Plenty of excellent ones stumble at free indirect style. Free indirect style solves much, but accentuates a problem inherent in all fictional narration: do the words these characters use seem the words they might use, or do they sound more like the author's?

When I wrote, 'Ted watched the orchestra through stupid

---

[4] Nabokov is a great creator of the kind of extravagant metaphors that the Russian formalists called 'estranging' or defamiliarising (a nutcracker has legs, a half-rolled black umbrella looks like a duck in deep mourning, and so on). The formalists liked the way that Tolstoy, say, insisted on seeing adult things – like war, or the opera – from a child's viewpoint, in order to make them look strange. But whereas the Russian formalists see this metaphorical habit as emblematic of the way that fiction does not refer to reality, is a self-enclosed machine (such metaphors are then jewels of the author's freakish, solipsistic art), I prefer the way that such metaphors, as in Pnin's 'leggy thing', refer deeply to reality: because they emanate from the characters themselves, and are fruits of free indirect style. Shklovksy wonders out aloud, in *Theory of Prose*, if Tolstoy got his technique of estrangement from French authors like Chateaubriand, but Cervantes seems much more likely – as when Sancho first arrives in Barcelona, and sees the galleys on the water, with their many oars, and metaphorically mistakes the oars for feet: 'Sancho couldn't imagine how those hulks moving about on top of the sea could have so many feet.' This is estranging metaphor as a branch of free indirect style; it makes the world look peculiar but it makes Sancho look very familiar. I return to this in paragraph 109.

tears', the reader had no difficulty in assigning 'stupid' to the character himself. But if I had written, 'Ted watched the orchestra through viscous, swollen tears', the adjectives would suddenly look annoyingly authorial, as if I were trying to find the fanciest way of describing those tears.

Take John Updike in his novel *Terrorist*. On the third page of his book, he has his protagonist, a fervid eighteen-year-old American Muslim called Ahmad, walk to school along the streets of a fictionalised New Jersey town. Since the novel has hardly begun, Updike must work to establish the quiddity of his character:

> Ahmad is eighteen. This is early April; again green is sneaking into the stony city's earthy crevices. He looks down from his new height and thinks that to the insects unseen in the grass he would be, if they had a consciousness like his, God. In the year past he has grown three inches, to six feet – more materialist forces, working their will upon him. He will not grow any taller, he thinks, in this life or the next. *If there is a next,* an inner devil murmurs. What evidence beyond the Prophet's blazing and divinely inspired words proves that there is a next? Where would it be hidden? Who would forever stoke its boilers? What infinite source of energy would maintain opulent Eden, feeding its dark-eyed houris, swelling its heavy-hanging fruits, renewing the streams and splashing fountains, in which God, as described in the ninth sura of the Qur'an, takes eternal pleasure? What of the second law of thermodynamics?

Ahmad is walking along the street, looking about, and thinking: the classic post-Flaubertian novelistic activity. The first few lines are routine enough. Then Updike wants to make the thought theological, so he effects an uneasy transition: 'He will not grow any taller, he thinks, in this life or the next. *If there is a next*, an inner devil murmurs.' It seems very unlikely that a schoolboy thinking about how much he had grown in the last year would think: 'I shall not grow any taller, in this life or the next.' The words 'or the next' are there just to feed Updike a chance to write about the Islamic idea of heaven. We are only four pages in, and any attempt to follow Ahmed's own voice has been abandoned: the phrasing, syntax and lyricism are Updike's, not Ahmad's ('Who would forever stoke its boilers?') The penultimate line is telling: 'in which God, *as described in the ninth sura of the Qur'an*, takes eternal pleasure.' (My italics.) How willing Henry James was, by contrast, to let us inhabit Maisie's mind, and how much he squeezed into that single adverb, 'embarrassingly'. But Updike is unsure about entering Ahmad's mind, and crucially, unsure about *our* entering Ahmad's mind, and so he plants his big authorial flags all over his mental site. So he has to identify exactly which sura refers to God, although Ahmad would know where this appears, and would have no need to remind himself.[5]

---

[5] As soon as we imagine a Christian version of this narration, we can gauge Updike's awkward alienation from his character. Imagine a devout Christian schoolboy walking along, and the text going something like this: 'And wouldn't His will always be done, as described in the fourth line of the Lord's Prayer?' Free indirect style exists precisely to *get around* such clumsiness.

On the one hand, the author wants to have his or her own words, wants to be the master of a personal style; on the other hand, narrative bends towards its characters and their habits of speech. The dilemma is most acute in first-person narration, which is generally a nice hoax: the narrator pretends to speak to us, while in fact the author is writing to us, and we go along with the deception happily enough. Even Faulkner's narrators in *As I Lay Dying* rarely sound much like children or illiterates.

But the same tension is present in third-person narration, too: who really thinks that it is Leopold Bloom, in the midst of his stream-of-consciousness, who notices 'the flabby gush of porter' as it is poured into a drain, or appreciates 'the buzzing prongs' of a fork in a restaurant – and in such fine words? These exquisite perceptions and beautifully precise phrases are Joyce's, and the reader has to make a treaty, whereby we accept that Bloom will sometimes sound like Bloom and sometimes sound more like Joyce.

This is as old as literature: Shakespeare's characters sound like themselves and always like Shakespeare, too. It is not really Cornwall who wonderfully calls Gloucester's eye a 'vile jelly' before he rips it out – though Cornwall speaks the words – but Shakespeare, who has provided the phrase.

23

A contemporary writer like David Foster Wallace wants to push this tension to the limit. He simultaneously writes from within his characters' voices and writes over them, and does this in order to explore larger, if more abstract, questions of language. In this passage from his story 'The Suffering Channel', he evokes the ruined argot of Manhattan mediaspeak:

The other *Style* piece the associate editor had referred to concerned The Suffering Channel, a wide grid cable venture that Atwater had gotten Laurel Manderley to do an end run and pitch directly to the editor's head intern for WHAT IN THE WORLD. Atwater was one of three full time salarymen tasked to the WITW feature, which received .75 editorial pages per week, and was the closest any of the BSG weeklies got to freakshow or tabloid, and was a bone of contention at the very highest levels of *Style*. The staff size and large font specs meant that Skip Atwater was officially contracted for one 400 word piece every three weeks, except the juniormost of the WITW salarymen had been on half time ever since Eckleschafft-Bod had forced Mrs Anger to cut the editorial budget for everything except celebrity news, so in reality it was more like three finished pieces every eight weeks.

Here is another example of what I called 'unidentified free indirect style'. As in the Chekhov story, the language hovers around the viewpoint of the character (the journalist Atwater), but really emanates from a kind of 'village chorus' – it is an amalgam of the kind of language we might expect this particular community to speak if they were telling the story.

In Wallace's case, the language of his unidentified narration is hideously ugly, and painful for more than a page or two. No analogous problem arose for Chekhov and Verga, because they were not faced with the saturation of language by mass media. But in America, things are different: Dreiser in *Sister Carrie* (published in 1900) and Sinclair Lewis in *Babbitt* (1923) take care to reproduce in full the advertisements and business letters and commercial fliers they want novelistically to report on.

The risky tautology inherent in the contemporary writing project has begun: in order to evoke a debased language (the debased language your character might use), you must be willing to represent that mangled language in your text; and perhaps thoroughly debase your own language. Pynchon, DeLillo, David Foster Wallace are to some extent Lewis's heirs (probably in this respect only),[6] and Wallace pushes to parodic extremes his full-immersion method: he does not flinch at narrating twenty or thirty pages in the style quoted above. His fiction prosecutes an intense argument about the decomposition of language in America, and he is not afraid to decompose – and discompose – his own style in the interests of making us live through this linguistic America with him. 'This is America, you live in it; you let it happen,' as Pynchon writes in *The Crying of Lot 49*. Whitman calls America 'the greatest poem', but if this is the case then America may represent a mimetic danger to the writer, the bloating of one's own poem with that rival poem, America. Auden frames the general

---

[6] That's to say, they are to some extent old-fashioned American realists, despite their postmodern credentials: their language is mimetically full of America's language.

problem well in his poem 'The Novelist': the poet can dash forward like a hussar, he writes, but the novelist must slow down, learn how to be 'plain and awkward', and must 'Become the whole of boredom'. In other words, the novelist's job is to become, to impersonate what he describes, even when the subject itself is debased, vulgar, boring. David Foster Wallace is very good at becoming the whole of boredom.

25

So there is a tension basic to stories and novels: can we reconcile the author's perceptions and language with the character's perception and language? If the author and character are absolutely merged, as in the passage from Wallace above, we get, as it were, 'the whole of boredom' – the author's corrupted language just mimics an actually existing corrupted language we all know too well, and are in fact quite desperate to escape. But if author and character get too separated, as in the Updike passage, we feel the cold breath of an alienation over the text, and begin to resent the over-'literary' efforts of the stylist. The Updike is an example of aestheticism (the author gets in the way); the Wallace is an example of apparent anti-aestheticism (the character is all): but both examples are really species of the same aestheticism, which is at bottom the strenuous display of *style*.

26

So the novelist is always working with at least three languages. There is the author's own language, style, perceptual equipment, and so on; there is the character's presumed language, style, perceptual equipment, and so on; and there is what we could call the language of the world – the language which fiction inherits before it gets to turn it into novelistic style, the language of daily speech, of newspapers, of offices, of advertising, of the blogosphere and text messaging. In this sense, the novelist is a triple-writer, and the contemporary novelist now feels especially the pressure of this tripleness, thanks to the omnivorous presence of the third horse of this troika, the language of the world, which has invaded our subjectivity, our intimacy, the intimacy that James thought should be the proper quarry of the novel, and which he called (in a troika of his own) 'the palpable present-*intimate*'.[7]

27

Another example of the novelist writing over his character occurs (briefly), in Saul Bellow's *Seize the Day*. Tommy Wilhelm, the out-of-work salesman down on his luck, neither much of an aesthete nor an intellectual, is anxiously watching the board at a Manhattan commodity exchange. Next to him, an old hand, named Mr Rappaport, is smoking a cigar. 'A long perfect ash formed on the end of the cigar, the white ghost of the leaf with all its veins and its fainter pungency. It was ignored, in its beauty, by the old man. For it was beautiful. Wilhelm he ignored as well.'

It is a gorgeous, musical phrase, and characteristic of both Bellow and modern fictional narrative. The fiction slows down to draw our attention to a potentially neglected surface

---

[7] Letter to Sarah Orne Jewett, 5 October 1901.

or texture – an example of a 'descriptive pause',[8] familiar to us when a novel halts its action and the author says, in effect, 'now I am going to tell you about the town of N., which was nestled in the Carpathian foothills', or 'Jerome's house was a large dark castle, set in fifty thousand acres of rich grazing land.' But at the same time it is a detail apparently seen not by the author – or not only by the author – but by a character. And this is what Bellow wobbles on; he admits an anxiety endemic to modern narrative, and which modern narrative tends to elide. The ash is noticed, and then Bellow comments: 'It was ignored, in its beauty, by the old man. For it was beautiful. Wilhelm he ignored as well.' *Seize the Day* is written in a very close third-person narration, a free indirect style that sees most of the action from Tommy's viewpoint. Bellow seems here to imply that Tommy notices the ash, because it was beautiful, and that Tommy, also ignored by the old man, is also in some way beautiful. But the fact that Bellow tells us this is surely a concession to our implied objection: how and why would Tommy notice this ash, and notice it so well, in *these* fine words? To which Bellow replies, anxiously, in effect: 'Well, you might have thought Tommy incapable of such finery, but he really did notice this fact of beauty; and that is because he is somewhat beautiful himself.'

28

The tension between the author's style and his characters' style becomes acute when three elements coincide: when a

---

[8] This is Gérard Genette's term, from *Narrative Discourse* (1980).

notable stylist is at work, like Bellow or Joyce; when that stylist also has a commitment to following the perceptions and thoughts of his or her characters (a commitment usually organised by free indirect style or its offspring, stream-of-consciousness); and when the stylist has an especial interest in the rendering of detail.

Stylishness; free indirect style; and detail: I have described Flaubert, whose work opens up, and tries to solve, this tension, and who is really its founder.

FLAUBERT AND MODERN NARRATIVE

29

Novelists should thank Flaubert the way poets thank spring: it all begins again with him. There really is a time before Flaubert and a time after him. Flaubert decisively established what most readers and writers think of as modern realist narration, and his influence is almost too familiar to be visible. We hardly remark of good prose that it favours the telling and brilliant detail; that it privileges a high degree of visual noticing; that it maintains an unsentimental composure and knows how to withdraw, like a good valet, from superfluous commentary; that it judges good and bad neutrally; that it seeks out the truth, even at the cost of repelling us; and that the author's fingerprints on all this are, paradoxically, traceable but not visible. You can find some of this in Defoe or Austen or Balzac, but not all of it until Flaubert.

Take the following passage, in which Frédéric Moreau, the hero of *Sentimental Education*, wanders through the Latin Quarter, alive to the sights and sounds of Paris:

He sauntered idly up the Latin Quarter, usually bustling with life but now deserted, for the students had all gone home. The great walls of the colleges looked grimmer than ever, as if the silence had made them longer; all sorts of peaceful sounds could be heard, the fluttering of wings in bird-cages, the whirring of a lathe, a cobbler's hammer; and the old-clothes men, in the middle of the street, looking hopefully but in vain at every window. At the back of the deserted cafés, women behind the bars yawned between their untouched bottles; the newspapers lay unopened on the reading-room tables; in the laundresses' workshops the washing quivered in the warm draughts. Every now and then he stopped at a bookseller's stall; an omnibus, coming down the street and grazing the pavement, made him turn round; and when he reached the Luxembourg he retraced his steps.

This was published in 1869, but might have appeared in 1969; many novelists still sound essentially the same. Flaubert seems to scan the streets indifferently, like a camera. Just as when we watch a film we no longer notice what has been excluded, what is just outside the edges of the camera-frame, so we no longer notice what Flaubert chooses *not* to notice. And we no longer notice that what he *has* selected is not of course casually scanned but quite savagely chosen, that each detail is almost frozen in its gel of chosenness. How superb and magnificently isolate these details are – the women yawning, the unopened newspapers, the washing quivering in the warm air.

The reason that we don't, at first, notice how carefully Flaubert is selecting his details, is because Flaubert is working very hard to obscure this labour from us, and is keen to hide the question of who is doing all this noticing: Flaubert or Frédéric? Flaubert was explicit about this. He wanted the reader to be faced with what he called a smooth wall of apparently impersonal prose, the details simply amassing themselves like life. 'An author in his work must be like God in the universe, present everywhere and visible nowhere,' he famously wrote in one of his letters, in 1852. 'Art being a second nature, the creator of that nature must operate with analogous procedures: let there be felt in every atom, every aspect, a hidden, infinite impassivity. The effect on the spectator must be a kind of amazement. How did it all come about!'

To this end, Flaubert perfected a technique that is essential to realist narration: the confusing of habitual detail with dynamic detail. Obviously, in that Paris street, the women cannot be yawning for the same length of time as the washing is quivering or the newspapers lying on the tables. Flaubert's details belong to different time-signatures, some instantaneous and some recurrent, yet they are smoothed together as if they are all happening simultaneously.

The effect is lifelike – in a beautifully artificial way. Flaubert manages to suggest that these details are somehow at once important and unimportant: important because they have been noticed by him and put down on paper, and unimportant because they are all jumbled together, seen as if out of the corner of the eye; they seem to come at us 'like life'. From this flows a great deal of modern story-telling, such as war reportage. The crime writer and war reporter merely increase the extremity of this contrast between important and unimportant detail, converting it into a tension between the awful and the regular: a soldier dies while nearby a little boy goes to school.

31

Different time-signatures were not Flaubert's invention, of course. There have always been characters doing something while something else is going on. In Book 22 of *The Iliad*, Hector's wife is at home warming his bath though he has in fact died moments before; Auden praised Breughel, in 'Musée des Beaux Arts', for noticing that, while Icarus fell, a ship was calmly moving on through the waves, unnoticing. In the Dunkirk section of Ian McEwan's *Atonement*, the protagonist, a British soldier retreating through chaos and death towards Dunkirk, sees a barge going by. 'Behind him, ten miles away, Dunkirk burned. Ahead, in the prow, two boys were bending over an upturned bike, mending a puncture perhaps.'

Flaubert differs a bit from those examples in the *way* he insists on driving together short-term and long-term occurrences. Breughel and McEwan are describing two very different things happening at the same time; Flaubert is asserting a temporal impossibility: that the eye – his eye, or Frédéric's eye – can witness, in one visual gulp as it were, sensations and occurrences that must be happening at different speeds and at different times. In *Sentimental Education*, when the 1848 revolution comes to Paris and the soldiers are firing on everyone and all is mayhem: 'he ran all the way to the Quai Voltaire. An old man in his shirt-sleeves was weeping at an open window, his eyes raised towards the sky. The Seine was flowing peacefully by. The sky was blue; birds were singing in the Tuileries.' Again, the one-off occurrence of the old man at the window is dropped into the longer-term occurrences, as if they all belonged together.

32

From here, it is a small leap to the insistence, familiar in modern war reporting, that the awful and the regular will be noticed at the same time – by the fictional hero, and/or by the writer – and that in some way *there is no important difference between the two experiences*: all detail is somewhat numbing, and strikes the traumatised voyeur in the same way. Here, again, is *Sentimental Education*:

> There was firing from every window overlooking the square; bullets whistled through the air; the fountain had been pierced, and the water, mingling with blood, spread in puddles on the ground. People slipped in the mud on clothes, shakos, and weapons; Frédéric felt something soft under his foot; it was the hand of a sergeant in a grey overcoat who was lying face down in the gutter. Fresh groups of workers kept coming up, driving the fighters towards the guard-house. The firing became more rapid. The wine-merchants' shops were open, and every now and then somebody would go in to smoke a pipe or drink a glass of beer, before returning to fight. A stray dog started howling. This raised a laugh.

The moment that strikes us as decisively modern in that passage is 'Frédéric felt something soft under his foot; it was the hand of a sergeant in a grey overcoat.' First the calm, terrible anticipation ('something soft'), and then the calm, terrible validation ('it was the hand of a sergeant'), the writing refusing to become involved in the emotion of the material. Ian McEwan systematically uses the same technique in his Dunkirk section, and so does Stephen Crane – who read *Sentimental Education* – in *The Red Badge of Courage*:

> He was being looked at by a dead man who was seated with his back against a columnlike tree. The corpse was dressed in a uniform that once had been blue, but was now faded to a melancholy shade of green. The eyes, staring at the youth, had changed to the dull hue to be seen on the side of a dead fish. The mouth was open. Its red had changed to an appalling yellow. Over the gray skin of the face ran little ants. One was trundling a sort of a bundle along the upper lip.

This is even more 'cinematic' than Flaubert (and film, of course, borrows this technique from the novel). There is the calm horror ('the dull hue to be seen on the side of a dead fish'). There is the zoom-like action of the lens, as it gets closer and closer to the corpse. But the reader is getting closer and closer to the horror, while the prose is simultaneously moving further and further back, insisting on its anti-sentimentality. There is the modern commitment to detail itself: the protagonist seems to be noticing so much, recording everything! ('One was trundling a sort of bundle along the upper lip.' Would any of us actually see as much?)

And there are the different time-signatures: the corpse will
be dead forever, but on his face, life goes on; the ants are
busily indifferent to human mortality.[9]

---

[9] The ants crawling across the face represent almost a cliché of cinematic
grammar. Think of the ants on the hand in Buñuel's *Un chien andalou*,
or on the ear at the start of David Lynch's *Blue Velvet*.

FLAUBERT AND THE RISE OF THE FLÂNEUR

33

Flaubert can drive together his time-signatures because French verb-forms allow him to use the imperfect past tense to convey both discrete occurrences ('he was sweeping the road') and recurrent occurrences ('every week he swept the road'). English is clumsier, and we have to resort to 'he was doing something' or 'he would do something' or 'he used to do something' – 'every week he would sweep the road' – to translate recurrent verbs accurately. But as soon as we do that in English, we have given the game away, and are admitting the existence of different temporalities. In *Contre Sainte-Beuve*, Proust rightly saw that this use of the imperfect tense was Flaubert's great innovation. And Flaubert founds this new style of realism on his use of the eye – the authorial eye, and the character's eye. I said that Updike's Ahmad, just walking along the street noticing things and thinking thoughts, was engaged in the classic post-Flaubertian novelistic activity. Flaubert's Frédéric is a forerunner of what would later be called the flâneur – the loafer, usually a young man, who walks the streets with no great urgency, seeing, looking, reflecting. We know this type from Baudelaire, from the all-seeing narrator of Rilke's autobiographical novel *The*

Notebooks of Malte Laurids Brigge, and from Walter Benjamin's writings about Baudelaire.

34

This figure is essentially a stand-in for the author, is the author's porous scout, helplessly inundated with impressions. He goes out into the world like Noah's dove, to bring a report back. The rise of this authorial scout is intimately connected to the rise of urbanism, to the fact that huge conglomerations of mankind throw at the writer – or the designated perceiver – large, bewilderingly various amounts of detail. Jane Austen is, essentially, a rural novelist, and London, as figured in *Emma*, is really just the village of Highgate. Her heroines never idly walk along, just thinking and looking: all their thought is intensely directed to the moral problem at hand. But when Wordsworth, at around the time the young Austen was writing, visits London in *The Prelude*, he immediately begins to sound like a flâneur – like a modern novelist:

> Here files of ballads dangle from dead walls,
> Advertisements of giant-size, from high
> Press forward in all colour on the sight . . .
> A travelling Cripple, by the trunk cut short.
> And stumping with his arms . . .
> The Bachelor that loves to sun himself,
> The military Idler, and the Dame . . .
> The Italian, with his Frame of Images
> Upon his head; with basket at his waist
> The Jew; the stately and slow-moving Turk
> With freight of slippers piled beneath his arm.

Wordsworth goes on to write that if we tire of 'random sights', we can find in the crowd 'all specimens of man':

> Through all the colours which the sun bestows,
> And every character of form and face,
> The Swede, the Russian; from the genial South,
> The Frenchman and the Spaniard; from remote
> America, the Hunter-Indian; Moors,
> Malays, Lascars, the Tartar and Chinese,
> And Negro Ladies in white muslin gowns.

Notice how Wordsworth, like Flaubert, adjusts the lens of his optic as he pleases: we have several lines of generalised cataloguing (the Swede, the Russian, the American, etc.), but we end with a sudden plucking of a single colour-contrast: 'And Negro Ladies in white muslin gowns.' The writer zooms in and out at will, but these details, despite their differences in focus and intensity, are pushed at us, as if by the croupier's stick, in one single heap.

35

Wordsworth is looking himself at these aspects of London. He is being a poet, writing about himself. The novelist wants to record details like this, too, but it is harder to act like a lyric poet in the novel, because you have to write through other people, and then we are returned to our basic novelistic tension: is it the novelist who is noticing these things or the fictional character? In that first passage from *Sentimental Education*, is Flaubert doing a bit of nice Parisian scene-setting, with the reader assuming that Frédéric is seeing perhaps a *few* of the details in the paragraph while Flaubert sees all of them in his mind's eye; or is the entire passage essentially written in loose free indirect style, with the assumption that Frédéric notices *everything* Flaubert draws our attention to – the unopened newspapers, the women yawning, and so on? Flaubert's innovation was to make this question unnecessary, to so confuse author and flâneur that the reader unconsciously raises Frédéric up to the stylistic level of Flaubert: both must be pretty good, we decide, at noticing things, and we are content to leave it there.

Flaubert needs to do this because he is at once a realist and a stylist, a reporter and a poet manqué. The realist wants to record a great deal, to do a Balzacian number on Paris. But the stylist is not content with Balzacian jumble and verve; he wants to discipline this welter of detail, to turn it into immaculate sentences and images: Flaubert's letters speak of the effort of trying to turn prose into poetry.[10] We nowadays more or less assume, so strong is the post-Flaubertian inflection of our era, that a fancy stylist must sometimes write over his or her characters (as in the examples from Updike and from Saul Bellow); or that they may

---

[10] The differences between Balzacian and Flaubertian realism are three-fold: first, Balzac of course notices a great deal in his fiction, but the emphasis is always on abundance rather than intense selectivity of detail. Second, Balzac has no especial commitment to free indirect style or authorial impersonality, and feels wonderfully free to break in as the author/narrator, with essays and digressions and bits of social information. (He seems decidedly eighteenth-century in this respect.) Third, and following on from these two differences: he has no distinctively Flaubertian interest in blurring the question of *who* is noticing all this stuff. For these reasons, I see Flaubert and not Balzac as the real founder of modern fictional narrative.

appoint a surrogate: Humbert Humbert famously announces that he has a fancy prose style, as a way, surely, of explaining his creator's overdeveloped prose; Bellow likes to inform us that his characters are 'first-class noticers'.

36

By the time the Flaubertian innovations have reached a novelist like Christopher Isherwood, writing in the 1930s, they have been polished to high technical shine. *Goodbye to Berlin,* published in 1939, has a famous early statement: 'I am a camera with its shutter open, quite passive, recording, not thinking. Recording the man shaving at the window opposite and the woman in the kimono washing her hair. Some day, all this will have to be developed, carefully printed, fixed.' Isherwood makes good on his claim in a scene-setting passage like this, from the opening of the chapter entitled 'The Nowaks':

> The entrance to the Wassertorstrasse was a big stone archway, a bit of old Berlin, daubed with hammers and sickles and Nazi crosses and plastered with tattered bills which advertised auctions or crimes. It was a deep shabby cobbled street, littered with sprawling children in tears. Youths in woollen sweaters circled waveringly across it on racing bikes and whooped at girls passing with milk-jugs. The pavement was chalk-marked for the hopping game called Heaven and Earth. At the end of it, like a tall, dangerously sharp, red instrument, stood a church.

Isherwood asserts even more flagrantly than Flaubert a randomness of detail, while trying even harder than Flaubert to disguise that randomness: this is exactly the formalisation you would expect of a literary style, once radical seventy years before, that is now decomposing a bit into a familiar way of ordering reality on the page – a set of handy rules, in effect. Posing as a camera who simply records, Isherwood seems merely to turn a wide bland gaze to the Wassertor-strasse: there, he says, is an archway, a street littered with children, some youths on bikes and girls with milk-jugs. Just a quick look. But, like Flaubert, only much more assertively, Isherwood insists on slowing down dynamic activity, and freezing habitual occurrence. The street may well be littered with children, but they cannot all be 'in tears' all the time. Likewise the cycling youths and the walking milk-girls, who are presented as part of the habitual furniture of the place. On the other hand, the tattered bills and the ground marked with the children's game are plucked by the author from their quiescence, and made temporally noisy: they flash at us, suddenly, but they belong to a different time-signature than the children and youths.

37

The more one looks at this rather wonderful piece of writing, the less it seems 'a slice of life', or a camera's easy swipe, than a very careful ballet. The passage begins with an entrance: the entrance of the chapter. The reference to hammers and sickles and Nazi crosses introduces a note of menace, which is completed by the sardonic reference to commercial bills advertising 'auctions or crimes': this may be commerce but it is uncomfortably close to the political graffiti – after all, isn't auction and crime what politicians, especially the kind involved in communist or fascist activities, do? They sell us things and commit crimes. The Nazi 'crosses' nicely link us to the children's game called Heaven and Earth, and to the church, except that, threateningly enough, everything is inverted: the church no longer looks like a church but like a red instrument (a pen, a knife, an instrument of torture, the 'red' the colour of both blood and radical politics), while the 'cross' has been taken over by the Nazis. Given this inversion, we understand why Isherwood wants to top and tail this paragraph with the Nazi crosses at the start and the church at the end: each changes place in the course of a few lines.

38

So the narrator who promised that he was a mere camera, quite passive, recording, not thinking, is selling us a false-hood? Only in the sense that Robinson Crusoe's claim to be telling a true story is a falsehood: the reader is happy enough to efface the labour of the writer in order to believe two further fictions: that the narrator was somehow 'really there' (as in fact Isherwood, was, living in Berlin in the 1930s), and that the narrator is not really a writer. Or rather, what Flaubert's flâneur tradition tries to establish is that the narrator (or designated authorial scout) *is at once a kind of writer and not really a writer.* A writer by temperament but not by trade. A writer because he notices so much, so well; not really a writer because he is not expending any labour to put it down on the page, and after all is really noticing no more than you and I would see.

This solution to the tension between the style of the author and the style of the character presents a paradox. It announces, in effect: 'We moderns have all become writers, and all have highly sophisticated eyes for detail; but life is not actually as "literary" as this implies, because we don't have to worry too much about how such detail gets onto the page.' The tension between the style of the author and the style of the character disappears because literary style itself is made to disappear: and literary style is made to disappear through literary means.

39

Flaubertian realism, like most fiction, is both lifelike and artificial.[11] It is lifelike because detail really does hit us, especially in big cities, in a tattoo of randomness. And we do exist in different time-signatures. Suppose I am walking down a street. I am aware of many noises, much activity, a police siren, a building being demolished, the scrape of a shop door. Different faces and bodies stream past me. And as I pass a café, I catch the eye of a woman, who is sitting alone. She looks at me, I at her. A moment of pointless, vaguely erotic urban connection, but the face reminds me of someone I once knew, a girl with just the same kind of dark hair, and sets a train of thought going. I walk on, but that particular face in the café glows in my memory, is held there, and is being temporally preserved, while around me noise and activities are not being similarly preserved – are entering and

---

[11] I return to the question of artifice and lifelikeness in 'Truth, Convention, Realism', paragraphs 111–122.

leaving my consciousness. The face, you could say, is playing at 4/4, while the rest of the city is humming along more quickly at 6/8.

The artifice lies in the *selection* of detail. In life, we can swivel our heads and eyes, but in fact we are like helpless cameras. We have a wide lens, and must take in whatever comes before us. Our memory selects for us, but not much like the way literary narrative selects. Our memories are aesthetically untalented.

DETAIL

'But it's not possible any other way; only in the details can we understand the essential, as books and life have taught me. One needs to know every detail, since one can never be sure which of them is important, and which word shines out from behind things.'[12]

40

In 1985, the mountaineer Joe Simpson, 21,000 feet up in the Andes, fell off an ice ledge and broke his leg. Dangling uselessly from his ropes, he was left for dead by his climbing partner. Into his head, unbidden, came the Boney M song 'Brown Girl in the Ring'. He had never liked the song, and was infuriated at the thought of dying to this particular soundtrack.

In literature, as in life, death is often attended by apparent irrelevance, from Falstaff babbling of green fields, to Balzac's Lucien de Rubempré noticing architectural details just before taking his life (in *Splendeurs et misères des courtisanes*), to

---

[12] Sándor Márai, *Embers*, trans. Carol Brown Janeway (translation from the German version, 2001).

Prince Andrew on his deathbed dreaming of a trivial conversation in *War and Peace*, to Joachim in *The Magic Mountain* moving his arm along the blanket 'as if he were collecting or gathering something'. Proust implies that such irrelevance will always attend our deaths, because we are never prepared for them; we never think of our death as likely to occur 'this very afternoon'. Instead:

> One insists on one's daily outing so that in a month's time one will have had the necessary ration of fresh air; one has hesitated over which coat to take, which cabman to call; one is in the cab, the whole day lies before one, short because one must be back home early, as a friend is coming to see one; one hopes that it will be as fine again tomorrow; and one has no suspicion that death, which has been advancing within one on another plane, has chosen precisely this particular day to make its appearance, in a few minutes' time, more or less at the moment when the carriage reaches the Champs-Elysées.[13]

An example that comes close to Joe Simpson's experience occurs at the end of Chekhov's story 'Ward 6'. The doctor, Ragin, is dying: 'A herd of deer, extraordinarily beautiful and graceful, which he had read about the day before, ran past him; then a peasant woman reached out to him with a certified letter ... Mikhail Averyanych said something. Then everything vanished and Andrei Yefimych lost consciousness forever.' The peasant woman with the certified letter is a bit too 'literary' (the grim reaper's summons, etc.); but that herd of deer!

---

[13] Proust, *The Guermantes Way*, Part 2, Chapter 1.

How lovely the simplicity with which Chekhov, deep inside his character's mind, does not say 'he thought of the deer he had been reading about' or even 'he saw in his mind the deer he had been reading about', but just calmly asserts that the deer 'ran past him'.

41

On 28 March 1941, Virginia Woolf loaded her pockets with stones and walked into the River Ouse. Her husband, Leonard Woolf, was obsessively punctilious, and had kept a journal every day of his adult life, in which he recorded daily menus and car mileage. Apparently, nothing was different on the day his wife committed suicide: he entered the mileage for his car. But on this day the paper is obscured by a smudge, writes his biographer, Victoria Glendinning, 'a brownish-yellow stain which has been rubbed or wiped. It could be tea or coffee or tears. The smudge is unique in all his years of neat diary-keeping.'

The fictional detail closest in spirit to Leonard Woolf's smudged journal describes the last hours of Thomas Buddenbrooks. Thomas's sister, Frau Permaneder, has been keeping a deathbed vigil. Passionate but stoical, she gives way at one moment to her grief, and sings a prayer: 'Come, Lord, receive his failing breath.' But she has forgotten that she does not know the whole verse, falters, 'and had to make up for her abrupt end by the increased dignity of her manner'. Everyone is embarrassed. Then Thomas dies and Frau Permaneder flings herself to the ground and weeps bitterly. A second later, control has been reasserted: 'Her face still streamed with tears, but she was soothed and comforted and entirely herself as she rose to her feet and began straightway to occupy her mind with the announcement of the death – an enormous number of elegant cards, which must be ordered at once.' Life returns to busyness and routine after the tearing of death. A commonplace. But the selection of that adjective 'elegant' is subtle; the bourgeois order stirs to life with its 'elegant' cards, and Mann suggests that this class retains faith in the solidity and grace of objects, clings to them indeed.

42

In 1960, during the presidential election, Richard Nixon and John F. Kennedy fought the first ever televised debate. It is often said that the sweating Nixon 'lost' because he had a five o'clock shadow, and looked sinister.

People thought they knew what Richard Nixon looked like, until he was placed alongside the fairer Kennedy, and the television lights blazed. Then he looked different. Likewise, the married Anna Karenina meets Vronsky on the night train from Moscow to Petersburg. By morning, something important has changed, but is as yet not properly acknowledged by her. To evoke this, Tolstoy has Anna notice her husband, Karenin, in a new light. Karenin has come to meet Anna at the station, and the first thing she thinks is: 'Oh, mercy! Why have his ears become like that?' Her husband looks cold and imposing, but above all it is the ears that suddenly seem strange – 'his ears whose cartilages propped up the brim of his round hat of black felt'.

43

Boney M, the single smudge, Nixon's shadow: in life as in literature, we navigate via the stars of detail. We use detail to focus, to fix an impression, to recall. We snag on it. In Isaac Babel's story 'My First Fee', a teenaged boy is telling a prostitute a tall tale. She is bored and sceptical, until he says, fancifully, that he took 'bronze promissory notes' to a woman. Suddenly, she is hooked.

44

Literature differs from life in that life is amorphously full of detail, and rarely directs us toward it, whereas literature teaches us to notice – to notice the way my mother, say, often wipes her lips just before kissing me; the drilling sound of a London cab when its diesel engine is flabbily idling; the way old leather jackets have white lines in them like the striations of fat in pieces of meat; the way fresh snow 'creaks' underfoot; the way a baby's arms are so fat that they seem tied with string (ah, the others are mine but that last example is from Tolstoy!).[14]

---

[14] It is from *Anna Karenina*, and is a nice example of self-plagiarism. In that novel, not one but two babies – Levin's and Anna's – are described as looking as if string is tied round their fat little arms. Likewise, in *David Copperfield*, Dickens likens Uriah Heep's open mouth to a post office, and Wemmick's open mouth, in *Great Expectations* – to a post office. Stendhal writes, in *The Red and the Black*, about how politics ruins a novel in the way a gunshot would spoil a music concert, and then repeats the image in *The Charterhouse of Parma*. Henry James wrote that Balzac, in his monkish devotion to his art was 'a Benedictine of the

This tutoring is dialectical. Literature makes us better noticers of life; we get to practise on life itself; which in turn makes us better readers of detail in literature; which in turn makes us better readers of life. And so on and on. You have only to teach literature to realise that most young readers are poor noticers. I know from my own old books, wantonly annotated twenty years ago when I was a student, that I routinely under-lined for approval details and images and metaphors that strike me now as commonplace, while serenely missing things which now seem wonderful. We grow, as readers, and twenty-year-olds are relative virgins. They have not yet read enough literature to be taught by it how to read it.

46

Writers can be like those twenty-year-olds, too – stuck at different floors of visual talent. As in all departments of aesthetics, there are levels of success in noticing. Some writers are modestly endowed noticers, others are stupendously observant. And there are plenty of moments in fiction when a writer seems to hold back, keeping a power in reserve: an

---

actual', a phrase he liked so much he used it later about Flaubert. Cormac McCarthy writes, in *Blood Meridian*: 'the blue cordilleras stood footed in their paler image on the sand', and returns to that lovely verb seven years later in *All the Pretty Horses*: 'Where a pair of herons stood footed to their long shadows.' Why shouldn't he? Such things are rarely examples of haste and more often proof that a style has achieved self-consistency. And that a kind of Platonic ideal has been reached – these are the best, and there-fore unsurpassable, words for these subjects.

ordinary observation is followed by a remarkable detail, a spectacular enrichment of observation, as if the writer had been, previously, just warming up, with the prose now suddenly opening like a day-lily.

47

How would we know when a detail seems really true? What guides us? The medieval theologian Duns Scotus gave the name 'thisness' (*haecceitas*) to individuating form. The idea was adapted by Gerard Manley Hopkins, whose poetry and prose is full of thisness: the 'lovely behaviour' of 'silk-sack clouds' ('Hurrahing in Harvest'); or 'the glassy peartree' whose leaves 'brush/ The descending blue; that blue is all in a rush/ With richness . . . ('Spring').

Thisness is a good place to start.

By thisness, I mean any detail that draws abstraction towards itself and seems to kill that abstraction with a puff of palpability, any detail that centres our attention with its concretion. Marlow, in *Heart of Darkness*, recalls a man dying at his feet, with a spear in his stomach, and how 'my feet felt so very warm and wet that I had to look down . . . my shoes were full; a pool of blood lay very still, gleaming dark-red under the wheel.'[15] The man lies on his back, looking up at Marlow anxiously, gripping the spear in his stomach as if it were 'something precious, with an air of being afraid I would try to take it away from him'. By thisness I mean the kind

---

[15] The image was heavily borrowed by Cormac McCarthy in *No Country for Old Men* (2005), where people are forever having their boots fill up with blood – usually their own, however

of exact palpabilities that Pushkin squeezes into the fourteen-line stanzas of *Eugene Onegin*: Eugene's country estate, for instance, which has not been touched for years, and where the unopened cupboards contain fruit liqueurs, 'a book of household calculations', an obsolete 'calendar for 1808', and where the billiards table is equipped with a 'blunt cue'.

By thisness I mean the precise brand of greenness – 'Kendal green' – that Falstaff swears, in *Henry IV Part 1*, clothed the men who attacked him: 'three misbegotten knaves in Kendal green came at my back and let drive at me.' There is something wonderfully absurd about 'Kendal green': it sounds as if the ambushing 'knaves' did not just jump out from behind bushes, but were somehow dressed *as* bushes! And Falstaff is lying. He saw no men dressed in Kendal green; it was too dark. The comedy of the specificity – already perhaps inherent in the very name – is doubled because it is a fiction posing as a specificity; and Hal, aware of this, presses Falstaff, reiterating the ridiculous precision: 'Why, how couldst thou know these men in Kendal green when it was so dark thou couldst not see thy hand?'

By thisness, I mean the moment when Emma Bovary fondles the satin slippers she danced in weeks before at the great ball at La Vaubyessard, 'the soles of which were yellowed with the wax from the dance floor'. By thisness I mean the cow-manure that Ajax slips in while racing at the grand funeral games, in Book 23 of *The Iliad* (thisness is often used to puncture ceremonies like funerals and dinners that are designed precisely to euphemise thisness: what Tolstoy calls making a bad smell in the drawing room).[16]

---

[16] From *The Death of Ivan Ilyich*; Tolstoy likens talking about death to someone making a bad smell in a drawing room.

By thisness I mean the single 'cherry-coloured twist' that the tailor of Gloucester, in Beatrix Potter's tale of the same name, has not yet sewn. (Reading this to my daughter recently, for the first time in thirty-five years, I was instantly returned, by the talismanic activity of that 'cherry-coloured twist', to a memory of my mother reading it to me. Beatrix Potter means the red satin that must be sewn around the eyelet of a buttonhole on a fancy coat. But perhaps the phrase was so magical to me then because it sounded so sweet: like a licorice or sherbet *twist* – a word that was still used, then, by confectioners.)

48

Because thisness is palpability, it will tend toward substance – cow-shit, red silk, the wax of a ballroom floor, a calendar for 1808, blood in a boot. But it can be a mere name or an anecdote; palpability can be represented in the form of an anecdote or piquant fact. In *A Portrait of the Artist as a Young Man*, Stephen Dedalus sees that Mr Casey's fingers can't be straightened out, 'and Mr Casey told him that he got those three cramped fingers making a birthday present for Queen Victoria'. Why is this detail, about making a birthday present for Queen Victoria, so alive? We begin with the comic specificity, the concrete allusion: if Joyce had only written 'and Mr Casey got cramped fingers making a birthday present', the detail would obviously be relatively flat, relatively vague. If he had written: 'he got those *three* cramped fingers making a birthday present for *Aunt Mary*', the details would be livelier, but why? Is specificity in itself satisfying? I think it is, and we expect such satisfaction from literature. We want names and numbers.[17] And the source of the comedy and liveliness here lies in a nice paradox of expectation and its denial: the sentence has insufficient detail in one area and over-specific detail in another. It is clearly inadequate to claim that Mr Casey got his permanently cramped fingers from making 'a birthday present': what titanic operation could possibly have crippled him like this? So our hunger for specificity is excited by this comic vagueness; and then Joyce deliberately feeds us too much specificity with the detail about the recipient. It is gratifying to have been given so much fact, but the fact about Queen Victoria, posing as specific, is really very mysterious, and flagrantly fails to answer the basic question: what was the present? (I am assuming, and therefore hardly mentioning, that making a present for *Queen Victoria* – rather than Aunt Mary – is inherently funny.) Joyce's sentence is thus made up of two mysterious details – the gift and its recipient – with the latter posing as the answer to the former mystery. The comedy is all to do with our desire for thisness in detail, and Joyce's determination to merely *pretend* to satisfy it. Queen Victoria, like Falstaff's fictional Kendal green, is represented as the detail that promises to illuminate the surrounding gloom; or, we might say, the fact that promises to ground the fiction. It *does* ground the fiction, in one sense: our attention

---

[17] Lawrence's story 'Odour of Chrysanthemums' begins like this: 'The small locomotive engine, Number 4, came clanking, stumbling down from Selston – with seven full wagons.' Ford Madox Ford, who published it in the *English Review* in 1911, said that the precision of the 'Number 4' and the 'seven' wagons, announced the presence of a real writer. 'The ordinary careless writer,' he said, 'would say "some small wagons". This man knows what he wants. He sees the scene of his story exactly.' See John Worthen's biography of *D. H. Lawrence: The Early Years, 1885–1912* (1991).

is surely drawn to the concretion. But in another sense, it is funny because it either is (like Kendal green) or seems (Queen Victoria) more fictional than the surrounding fiction.

49

I confess to an ambivalence about detail in fiction. I relish it, consume it, ponder it. Hardly a day goes by in which I don't remind myself of Bellow's description of Mr Rappaport's cigar: 'the white ghost of the leaf, with all its veins and its fainter pungency'. But I choke on too much detail, and find that a distinctively post-Flaubertian tradition fetishises it: the over-aesthetic appreciation of detail seems to raise, in a slightly different form, that tension between author and character we have already explored.

If the history of the novel can be told as the development of free indirect style, it can no less be told as the rise of detail. It is hard to recall for how long fictional narrative was in thrall to neo-classical ideals, which favoured the formulaic and the imitative, rather than the individual and the original.[18] Of course, original and individual detail can never

---

[18] A nice index of this can be found in Adam Smith's *Lectures on Rhetoric and Belles Lettres* (1762–3), in which he says that poetic and rhetorical description should be brief, to the point, and not lengthy. But, he goes on, 'it is often proper to Choose out some nice and Curious' detail. 'A Painter in Drawing a fruit makes the figure very striking if he not only gives it the form and Colour but also represents the fine down with which it is covered.' Smith recommends this in such a fresh and ingenuous way – as if he is saying, 'wouldn't it be a good idea to notice the fine down on a piece of fruit?' – that he makes the very concept of detail sound somewhat novel and new-fangled.

58

be suppressed: Pope and Defoe and even Fielding are full of what Blake called the 'minute particulars'. But it is impossible to imagine a novelist in 1770 saying what Flaubert said to Maupassant in 1870: 'There is a part of everything which is unexplored, because we are accustomed to using our eyes only in association with the memory of what people before us have thought of the thing we are looking at. Even the smallest thing has something in it which is unknown.'[19] J. M. Coetzee, in his novel *Elizabeth Costello*, has this to say about Defoe:

> The blue costume, the greasy hair, are details, signs of a moderate realism. Supply the particulars, allow the significations to emerge of themselves. A procedure pioneered by Daniel Defoe. Robinson Crusoe, cast upon the beach, looks around for his shipmates. But there are none. 'I never saw them afterwards, or any sign of them,' says he, 'except three of their hats, one cap, and two shoes that were not fellows.' 'Two shoes, not fellows': by not being fellows, the shoes have ceased to be footwear and become proofs of death, torn by the foaming seas off the feet of drowning men and tossed ashore. No large words, no despair, just hats and caps and shoes.

Coetzee's phrase 'moderate realism' describes a way of writing in which the kind of detail we are directed to does not yet have the kind of extravagant commitment to noticing and re-noticing, to novelty and strangeness, characteristic of modern novelists – an eighteenth-century regime, in which the cult of 'detail' has not yet really been established.

---

[19] Maupassant, 'The Novel', preface to *Pierre and Jean* (1888).

You can read *Don Quixote*, or *Tom Jones*, or Austen's novels and find very little of the detail Flaubert recommends. Austen gives us none of the visual furniture we find in Balzac or Joyce, and hardly ever stops to describe even a character's face. Clothes, climates, interiors, all are elegantly compressed and thinned. Minor characters in Cervantes, Fielding and Austen are theatrical, often formulaic, and are barely noticed, *in a visual sense*. Fielding quite happily describes two different characters in *Joseph Andrews* as having 'Roman noses'.

But for Flaubert, for Dickens, and for hundreds of novelists after them, the minor character is a delicious kind of stylistic challenge: how to make us see him, how to animate him, how to dab him with a little gloss? (Like Dora's cousin in *David Copperfield*, who is 'in the Life-Guards, with such long legs that he looked like the afternoon shadow of somebody else'.) Here is Flaubert's sidelong glance at a minor character at a ball, never seen again, in *Madame Bovary*:

There, at the top of the table, alone among all these women, stooped over his ample plateful, with his napkin tied around his neck like a child, an old man sat eating, drops of gravy dribbling from his lips. His eyes were bloodshot and he had a little pigtail tied up with a black ribbon. This was the Marquis's father-in-law, the old Duc de Laverdière, once the favourite of the Comte d'Artois . . . and he, so they said, had been the lover of Marie Antoinette, in between Monsieurs de Coigny and de Lauzun. He had led a tumultuous life of debauchery and dueling, of wagers made and women abducted, had squandered his fortune and terrified his whole family.

As so often, the Flaubertian legacy is a mixed blessing. Again, there is that strange burden of 'chosenness' we feel around Flaubert's details, and the implication of that chosenness for the novelist's characters – our sense that the selection of detail has become a poet's obsessive excruciation rather than a novelist's easy joy. (The flâneur – the hero who is both a writer and not a writer – solves this problem, or attempts to. But in the example above, Flaubert has no adequate surrogate, because his surrogate is Emma: so in effect this is the novelist, pure and simple, watching.) Here is Rilke, in *The Notebooks of Malte Laurids Brigge*, being excruciatingly exact about a blind man he has seen in the street: 'I had undertaken the task of imagining him, and was sweating from the effort . . . I understood that nothing about him was insignificant . . . his hat, an old, high-crowned, stiff felt hat, which he wore the way all blind men wear their hats: without any relation to the lines of the face, without the possibility of adding this feature to themselves and forming a new external unity: but merely as an arbitrary, extraneous object.'[20] Impossible to imagine a writer before Flaubert indulging in these theatrics ('was sweating from the effort')! What Rilke says about the blind man reads like a projection of his own sweaty literary anxieties onto the man: when no literary detail is insignificant, then perhaps indeed each will indeed fail to 'form a new external unity' and will be 'merely' an 'arbitrary, extraneous object'.

In Flaubert and his successors we have the sense that the ideal of writing is a procession of strung details, a necklace of noticings, and that this is sometimes an obstruction to seeing, not an aid.

---

[20] Rilke, *The Notebooks of Malte Laurids Brigge*, trans. Stephen Mitchell.

51

So during the nineteenth century, the novel became more *painterly*. In *La Peau de Chagrin*, Balzac describes a table-cloth 'white as a layer of newly fallen snow, upon which the place-settings rise symmetrically, crowned with blond rolls'. Cézanne said that all through his youth, 'I wanted to paint that, that tablecloth of new snow.'[21] Nabokov and Updike at times freeze detail into a cult of itself. Aestheticism is the great risk here, and also an exaggeration of the noticing eye. (There is so much detail in life that is not purely visual.) The Nabokov who writes of 'an elderly flower-girl, with carbon eyebrows and a painted smile, [who] nimbly slipped the plump torus of a carnation into the buttonhole of an intercepted stroller whose left jowl accentuated its royal fold as he glanced downward sideways at the coy insertion of the flower', becomes the Updike who notices the rain on a window thus: 'Its panes were strewn with drops that as if by amoebic decision would abruptly merge and break and jerkily run downward, and the window screen, like a sampler half-stitched, or a crossword puzzle invisibly solved, was inlaid erratically with minute, translucent tesserae of rain.'[22] It is significant that Updike likens the rainy window to a cross-word puzzle: both these writers, in this mode, sound as if they are setting us a puzzle.

Bellow notices superbly; but Nabokov wants to tell us

---

[21] Quoted in Maurice Merleau-Ponty, 'Cézanne's Doubt', in *Sense and Non-Sense* (1948).
[22] From Nabokov, 'First Love' (1925) and Updike, *Of the Farm* (1961). And one can hear how David Foster Wallace comes out of this tradition, too, even if he renders comically or ironically a level of obsessive detail that Updike renders more earnestly.

how important it is to notice. Nabokov's fiction is always becoming propaganda on behalf of good noticing, hence on behalf of itself. There are beauties that are not visual at all, and Nabokov has poorish eyes for those. How else to explain his dismissals of Mann, Camus, Faulkner, Stendhal, James? He judges them, essentially, for not being stylish enough, and for not being visually alert enough. The battle-line emerges clearly in one of his exchanges with the critic Edmund Wilson, who had been trying to get Nabokov to read Henry James. At last, Nabokov cast his eye over *The Aspern Papers*, but reported back to Wilson that James was sloppy with detail. When James describes the lit end of a cigar, seen from outside a window, he calls it a 'red tip'. But cigars don't have tips, says Nabokov. James wasn't *looking* hard enough. He goes on to compare James's writing to 'the weak blond prose' of Turgenev.[23]

A cigar, again! Here are two different approaches to the creation of detail. James, I think, would reply that first of all, cigars do have tips, and secondly, that there is no need, every time one describes a cigar, to do a Bellovian or Nabokovian job on it. That James was *incapable* of doing such a job – the implication of Nabokov's complaint – is easily disproved. But James is certainly not a Nabokovian writer; his notion of what constitutes a detail is more various, more impalpable, and finally more metaphysical than Nabokov's. James would probably argue that while we should indeed try to be the kind of writer on whom nothing is lost, we have no need to be the kind of writer on whom everything is found.

---

[23] *The Nabokov–Wilson Letters*, ed. Simon Karlinsky (1979).

52

There is a conventional modern fondness for quiet but 'telling' detail: 'The detective noticed that Carla's hairband was surprisingly dirty.' If there is such a thing as a telling detail, then there must be such a thing as an untelling detail, no? A better distinction might be between what I would call 'off-duty' and 'on-duty detail'; the off-duty detail is part of the standing army of life, as it were – it is always ready to be activated. Literature is full of such off-duty detail (James's red cigar tip would be an example).

But maybe 'off-duty' and 'on-duty' just rephrases the problem? Isn't off-duty detail essentially detail that is not as telling as its on-duty comrades? Nineteenth-century realism, from Balzac on, creates such an abundance of detail that the modern reader has come to expect of narrative that it will always contain a certain superfluity, a built-in redundancy, that it will *carry more detail than it needs*. In other words, fiction builds into itself a lot of surplus detail just as life is full of surplus detail. Suppose I were to describe a man's head like this: 'He had very red skin, and his eyes were bloodshot; his brow looked angry. There was a small mole on his upper lip.' The red skin and bloodshot eyes and angry skin tell us, perhaps, something about the man's disposition, but the mole seems 'irrelevant'. It's just 'there'; it is reality, it is just 'how he looked'.

53

But is this layer of gratuitous detail actually like life or just a trick? In his essay 'The Reality Effect',[24] Roland Barthes

---

[24] Collected in *The Rustle of Language*, trans. Richard Howard (1986).

essentially argues that 'irrelevant' detail is a code we no longer notice, and one that has little to do with how life really is. He discusses a passage by the historian Jules Michelet, in which Michelet is describing the last hours of Charlotte Corday in prison. An artist visits her and paints her portrait, and then 'after an hour and a half, there was a gentle knock at a little door behind her'. Then Barthes turns to Flaubert's description of Mme Aubain's room in *A Simple Heart*: 'Eight mahogany chairs were lined up against the white-painted wainscoting, and under the barometer stood an old piano loaded with a pyramid of boxes and cartons.' The piano, Barthes argues, is there to suggest bourgeois status, the boxes and cartons perhaps to suggest disorder. But why is the barometer there? The barometer denotes nothing; it is an object 'neither incongruous nor significant'; it is apparently 'irrelevant'. Its business is to denote reality, it is there to create the effect, the atmosphere of the real. It simply says: 'I am the real.' (Or if you prefer: 'I am realism.')

An object like the barometer, Barthes continues, is *supposed* to denote the real, but in fact all it does is signify it. In the Michelet passage, the little 'filler' of the knock at the door is the kind of thing that this writing 'puts in' to create the realistic 'effect' of time passing. Realism in general, it is implied, is just such a business of false denotation. The barometer is interchangeable with a hundred other items; realism is an artificial tissue of mere arbitrary signs. Realism offers the appearance of reality but is in fact utterly fake – what Barthes calls 'the referential illusion'.

In *Mythologies*, Barthes wittily pointed out that those laurel-leaf haircuts worn by the actors in Hollywood's 'Roman' films signify 'Romanness' in the way that Flaubert's barometer signifies 'realness'. In neither case is anything actually *real* being denoted. These are mere stylistic conventions, in the way that flares or the miniskirt have meaning only as part of a system of signification established by the fashion industry itself. The codes of fashion are entirely arbitrary. As far as he was concerned, literature was like fashion, because both systems make one read the signifying of things rather than their meaning.[25]

54

But Barthes is too quick to decide what is relevant and irrelevant detail. Why is the barometer irrelevant? If the barometer exists only to arbitrarily proclaim the real, why don't the piano and boxes, too? As A. D. Nuttall puts it in *A New Mimesis*, the barometer doesn't say 'I am the real' so much as 'Am I not just the sort of thing you would find in such a house?' It is neither incongruous nor especially significant, precisely because it is dully typical. There are plenty of houses that still have such barometers, and those barometers indeed tell us something about the kinds of houses they are in: middle class rather than upper class; a certain kind of conventionality; a musty devotion, perhaps, to second-rate heirlooms; and the barometer is *never right*, is it? What does this tell us? In Britain, of course, they are especially comical tools, since the weather is always the same: grey, a bit of rain. You would never need a barometer. In fact, barometers, you might say, are very good barometers of a certain middling status: barometers are very good barometers of themselves! (*That's* how they work, then.)

---

[25] *Système de la mode* (1967).

Anyway, one can accept Barthes's stylistic proviso without accepting his epistemological caveat: fictional reality is indeed made up of such 'effects', but realism can be an effect and still be true. It is only Barthes's sensitive, murderous hostility to realism that insists on this false division.

55

In Orwell's essay 'A Hanging' the writer watches the condemned man, walking towards the gallows, swerve to avoid a puddle. For Orwell, this represents precisely what he calls the 'mystery' of the life that is about to be taken: when there is no good reason for it, the condemned man is still thinking about keeping his shoes clean. It is an 'irrelevant' act (and a marvellous bit of noticing on Orwell's part). Now suppose this were not an essay but a piece of fiction. And indeed there has been a fair amount of speculation about the proportion of fact to fiction in such essays of Orwell's. The avoidance of the puddle would be precisely the kind of superb detail that, say, Tolstoy might flourish; *War and Peace* has an execution scene very close in spirit to Orwell's essay, and it may well be that Orwell basically cribbed the detail from Tolstoy. In *War and Peace*, Pierre witnesses a man being executed by the French, and notices that, just before death, the man adjusts the blindfold at the back of his head, because it is uncomfortably tight.[26] The avoidance of the puddle, the fiddling with the blindfold – these are what might be called irrelevant or superfluous details. They are not explicable; in fiction, they exist to denote precisely the

---

[26] *War and Peace*, Book Four, Chapter 11.

inexplicable. This is one of the 'effects' of realism, of 'realistic' style. But Orwell's essay, assuming it records an actual occurrence, shows us that such fictional effects are not merely conventionally irrelevant, or formally arbitrary, but have something to tell us about the *irrelevance of reality itself*. In other words, the category of the irrelevant or inexplicable exists in life, just as the barometer exists, in all its uselessness, in real houses. There was no logical reason for the condemned man to avoid the puddle. It was pure remembered habit. Life, then, will always contain an inevitable surplus, a margin of the gratuitous, a realm in which there is always more than we need: more things, more impressions, more memories, more habits, more words, more happiness, more unhappiness.

56

The barometer, the puddle, the adjustment of the blindfold, are not 'irrelevant'; they are significantly insignificant. In 'The Lady with the Little Dog', a man and a woman go to bed. After sex, the man calmly eats a melon: 'There was a watermelon on the table in the hotel room. Gurov cut himself a slice and unhurriedly began to eat it. At least half an hour passed in silence.' That is all Chekhov writes. He could have done it like this: 'Thirty minutes passed. Outside, a dog started barking, and some children ran down the street. The hotel manager yelled something. A door slammed.' These details would obviously be exchangeable with other, similar details; they are not crucial to anything. They would be there to make us feel that this is lifelike. Their insignificance is precisely their significance. And, as in the Michelet passage of which Barthes is so suspicious, one of the obvious reasons for the rise of this kind of significantly insignificant detail is that it is needed to evoke the passage of time, and fiction has a new and unique project in literature – the management of temporality. In ancient narratives, for instance, like Plutarch's Lives or the Bible stories, gratuitous detail is very hard to find. Mostly detail is functional or symbolic. Likewise, the ancient storytellers seem to feel no pressure to evoke a lifelike passing of 'real time' (Chekhov's thirty minutes). Time passes jerkily, swiftly: 'And Abraham rose up early in the morning, and saddled his ass, and took two of his young men with him, and Isaac his son, and clave the wood for the burnt offering, and rose up, and went unto the place of which God had told him. Then on the third day Abraham lifted up his eyes, and saw the place afar off.' Time lapses *between* the verses, invisibly, inaudibly, but nowhere on the page. Each new 'And' or 'Then' moves forward the action like those old station-clocks, whose big hands suddenly slip forward once a minute.

We have seen that Flaubert's method of different temporalities requires a combination of detail, some of which are relevant, some studiedly irrelevant. '*Studiedly* irrelevant' – we concede that there really is no such thing as irrelevant detail in fiction, even in realism, which tends to use such detail as a kind of padding, to make verisimilitude seem nice and comfy. You wastefully leave lights on in your home or hotel room when you aren't there, not to prove that you exist, but because *the margin of surplus itself* feels like life, feels in some curious way like being alive.

In 'The Dead', Joyce writes that Gabriel was his old aunts' favourite nephew: 'He was their favourite nephew, the son of their dead elder sister, Ellen, who had married T. J. Conroy of the Port and Docks.' This might not look like anything much, at first; perhaps one has to be familiar with a certain kind of petit bourgeois snobbery to appreciate it. But what a lot it tells us about the two sisters, in just a handful of words! It is the kind of detail that speeds on our knowledge of a character: a state of mind, a gesture, a stray word. It pertains to human and moral understanding – detail not as thisness but as knowledge.

Joyce drops into free indirect style at the very end of the sentence, to inhabit the collective mind of the proper and snobbish old ladies, who are 'caught' thinking about their brother-in-law's status. Imagine if the line went: 'He was their favourite nephew, Ellen and Tom's fine son.' The sentence would tell us nothing about the sisters. Instead, Joyce's point is that *inside their own minds, in their private voices*, they still think of their brother-in-law not as 'Tom', but as 'T. J. Conroy, of the Port and Docks'. They are proud of his attainment, of his substance in the world, even a little daunted by it. And that gnomic 'of the Port and Docks' functions like the birthday present for Queen Victoria: we don't know what T. J. Conroy did at the Port and Docks, and it is exquisitely difficult to know how grand a job at the Port and Docks could possibly be. (That is the comedy.) But Joyce – working in a manner exactly opposite to Updike in that passage from *Terrorist* – knows that to tell us any more about the Port and Docks would ruin the psychological truth: *this* status means something important to *these* women. It is enough to know that.

This sudden capturing of a central human truth, this moment when a single detail has suddenly enabled us to see a character's thinking (or lack of it), can be a branch of free indirect style, as in the example above. But not necessarily: it may be the novelist's observation from 'outside' the character (though it speeds us inside, of course). There is such a moment in *The Radetzky March*, when the old captain visits his dying servant, who is in bed, and the servant tries to click his naked heels together under the sheets . . . or in *The Possessed*, when the proud, weak governor, von Lembke, loses his control. Shouting at a group of visitors in his drawing room, he marches out, only to trip on the carpet. Standing still, he looks at the carpet and ridiculously yells, 'have it changed!' – and walks out . . . or when Charles Bovary returns with his wife from the grand ball at La Vaubyessard, which has so enchanted Emma, rubs his hands together and says: 'It's good to be home' . . . or in *Sentimental Education* when Frédéric takes his rather humble mistress to Fontainebleau. She is bored, but can tell that Frédéric is frustrated with her lack of culture. So in one of the galleries, she looks around at the paintings and, trying to say something knowing and impressive, merely exclaims: 'All this brings back memories!' . . . or when, after his divorce, Anna Karenina's husband, the stiff and joyless civil servant, goes around introducing himself with the line: 'You are acquainted with my grief?'

58

These details help us to 'know' Karenin or Bovary or Frédéric's mistress, but they also present a mystery. Years ago, my wife and I were at a concert given by the violinist Nadja Salerno-Sonnenberg. At a quiet, difficult passage of bowing, she frowned. Not the usual ecstatic moue of the virtuoso, it expressed sudden irritation. At the same moment, we invented entirely different readings. Claire later said to me: 'She was frowning because she wasn't playing that bit well enough.' I replied: 'No, she was frowning because the audience was so noisy.' A good novelist would have let that frown alone, and would have let our revealing comments alone, too: no need to smother this little scene in explanation.

Detail like this – that enters a character but refuses to explain that character – makes us the writer as well as the reader; we seem like co-creators of the character's existence. We have an *idea* of what is going through von Lembke's mind when he shouts 'Have it changed!', but there are several possible readings; we have an idea of Rosanette's awkwardness, but we can't know what exactly she means when she says 'All this brings back memories!' These characters are somehow very private, even as they artlessly expose themselves.

'The Lady with the Little Dog' is almost entirely composed of details that refuse to explain themselves, and this suits the story because it is about a love affair that brings a great happiness somewhat inexplicable to the lovers. A married man – and expert seducer – meets a married woman in Yalta; they go to bed. Why do at least thirty minutes go by in silence as Gurov eats his melon? Several reasons come to mind: and we fill that silence with *our* reasons. Later in the story, the confident seducer decides, in ways he cannot fully express, that this ordinary-looking woman from a small town means more to him than anyone he has ever loved. He journeys from Moscow to the woman's provincial town, and they meet at the local theatre. The orchestra, writes Chekhov, takes *a long time to tune*. (Again, no commentary is offered: we are free to assume that provincial orchestras are inexpert.) The lovers snatch a moment outside the auditorium, on the stairs. Above, two schoolboys watch them, smoking. Do the boys know what drama is happening beneath them? Are they indifferent? Are the lovers troubled by the surveillance of the schoolboys? Chekhov does not say.

The perfection of the detail has to do with symmetry: two malefactors have encountered two other malefactors, and each couple has nothing to do with the other.

A Chekhovian English writer, the modernist Henry Green, likes to further gag commentary, and delights in apparently misleading the reader. His novel *Caught* (1943) is set during the London Blitz, and concerns the Auxiliary Fire Service, the wartime brigade composed of civilians who, for various reasons, were not called up for fighting. The brigade in question is often incompetent; one day, called to a domestic fire, they manage to enter the wrong building – the house next to the one on fire. A day later, the district officer (a professional fireman), a man called Trant, recalls this debacle: 'Up at Number Fifteen, Trant's wife, as he left his quarters, promised him pork pie for dinner. This put Trant in mind of his sub officer who had made them a laughing stock the previous day, running about like a chicken that had its head cut off, with his Auxiliaries like a herd of sodding geese.' Now, why does pork pie 'put Trant in mind' of the earlier incident? Green feels no need to tell us. All we can do is surmise that Trant thinks something like: 'pork pie . . . dead pig . . . farmyard . . . chickens run around after they have been killed . . . that bloody mess yesterday when my men ran around like chickens with their heads cut off.' But what is laborious when written out in this Joycean manner is sparklingly

opaque when compressed into the swift, lip-zipped statement of Green's free indirect style. This seems very close to
how our minds do actually work.

But it may not be how Trant's mind worked at all. Perhaps
he thought: 'pork pie . . . yesterday's bloody mess . . . like a
chicken with its head cut off' – in that order?

CHARACTER

The punchline of the story relates to an American academic saying of Beckett, 'He doesn't give a fuck about people. He's an artist.' At this point Beckett raised his voice above the clatter of afternoon tea and shouted, 'But I *do* give a fuck about people! I *do* give a fuck!'[27]

59

There is nothing harder than the creation of fictional character. I can tell it from the number of apprentice novels I read that begin with descriptions of photographs. You know the style: 'My mother is squinting in the fierce sunlight and holding, for some reason, a dead pheasant. She is dressed in old-fashioned lace-up boots, and white gloves. She looks absolutely miserable. My father, however, is in his element, irrepressible as ever, and has on his head that grey velvet trilby from Prague I remember so well from my childhood.' The unpractised novelist cleaves to the static, because it is much easier to describe than the mobile: it is getting these

---

[27] *Beckett Remembering: Remembering Beckett*, ed. James and Elizabeth Knowlson (2006).

people out of the aspic of arrest and mobilised in a scene that is hard. When I encounter a prolonged ekphrasis like the parody above, I worry, suspecting that the novelist is clinging to a handrail and is afraid to push out.

60

But how to push out? How to animate the static portrait? Ford Madox Ford, in his book *Joseph Conrad: A Personal Remembrance*, writes wonderfully about getting a character up and running – what he calls 'getting a character *in*'. He says that Conrad himself 'was never really satisfied that he had really and sufficiently got his characters in; he was never convinced that he had convinced the reader; this accounting for the great lengths of some of his books.' I like this idea, that some of Conrad's novels are long because he couldn't stop fiddling, page after page, with the verisimilitude of his characters – it raises the spectre of an infinite novel. At least the apprentice writer, with his bundle of nerves, is in good company, then. Ford and Conrad loved a sentence from a Maupassant story, 'La Reine Hortense': 'He was a gentleman with red whiskers who always went first through a doorway.' Ford comments: 'that gentleman is so sufficiently got in that you need no more of him to understand how he will act. He has been "got in" and can get to work at once.'

Ford is right. Very few brushstrokes are needed to get a portrait walking, as it were; and – a corollary of this – the reader can get as much from small, short-lived, even rather flat characters as from large, round, towering heroes and heroines. To my mind, Gurov, the adulterer in 'The Lady with the Little Dog', is as vivid, as rich, and as sustaining as Gatsby or Dreiser's Hurstwood, or even Jane Eyre.

61

Let us think about this for a moment. A stranger enters a room. How do we immediately begin to take his measure? We look at his face, his clothing, for sure. This man, let us say, is middle-aged, still handsome, but going bald – he has a smooth space on the top of his head, fringed with flattened hair, which looks like a pale crop circle. Something about his carriage suggests a man who expects to be noticed; on the other hand, he smooths his hand over his head so often in the first few minutes that one suspects him of being a little uneasy about having lost that hair.

This man, let us say, is curious, because the top half of him is expensively turned out – a fine, pressed shirt, a good jacket – while the bottom half is slovenly: stained, creased trousers, old unpolished shoes. Does he expect, then, that people will only notice the top of him? Might this suggest a certain faith in his own theatrical ability to hold people's attention? (Keep them looking at your face.) Or perhaps his own life is similarly bifurcated? Perhaps he is ordered in some ways, disordered in others.

62

We can tell a great deal from a character by how he talks, and whom he talks to – how he bumps up against the world. People, as Edith Wharton said, are like other people's estates: we only know of them what abuts our own. Let us say that the man with dishevelled trousers enters a room in which are standing a man and a woman. He speaks first to the woman, and ignores the man. Ah, we say to ourselves, he is *that* kind of guy. But then the novelist reveals to us that the woman he is talking to is strikingly unattractive. And suddenly, the extraordinary capacity of the novel speaks: unlike film, say, the novel can tell us what a character is thinking. And at this moment, the novelist chooses to add, in free indirect style, no less: 'Mother, very traditional in her way, had always instructed him that a gentleman should talk first to the least attractive woman in the room, to make her feel at ease. Simple chivalry.'

The above would constitute no more than a paragraph.

63

In Antonioni's film *L'Eclisse*, the luminous Monica Vitti visits the Rome stock exchange, where her fiancé, played by Alain Delon, works. Delon points out a fat man who has just lost 50 million lire. Intrigued, she follows the man. He orders a drink at a bar, barely touches it, then goes to a café, where he orders an *acqua minerale*, which he again barely touches. He is writing something on a piece of paper, and leaves it on the table. We imagine that it must be a set of furious, melancholy figures. Vitti approaches the table, and sees that it is a drawing of a flower . . .

Who would not love this little scene? It is so delicate, so tender, so sidelong and lightly humorous, and the joke is so nicely on us. We had a stock idea of how the financial victim responds to catastrophe – collapse, despair, self-defenestration – and Antonioni confounded our expectations. The character slips through our changing perceptions, like a boat moving through canal-locks. We begin in misplaced certainty and end in placeless mystery.

The scene raises the question of what really constitutes a character. We know nothing more about this investor than this episode scene tells us; he has no continuing role in the film. Is he really a 'character' at all? Yet no one would dispute that Antonioni has revealed something sharp and deep about this man's temperament, and by extension about a certain human insouciance under pressure – or possibly, about a certain defensive will-to-insouciance under pressure. Something alive, human has been disclosed. So this scene demonstrates that narrative can and often does give us a vivid sense of a character without giving us a vivid sense of an individual. We don't know this particular man; but we know his particular behaviour at this moment.

64

A great deal of nonsense is written every day about characters in fiction – from the side of those who believe too much in character and from the side of those who believe too little. Those who believe too much have an iron set of prejudices about what characters are: we should get to 'know' them; they should not be 'stereotypes'; they should have an 'inside' as well as an outside, depth as well as surface; they should 'grow' and 'develop'; and they should be nice. So they should be pretty much like us. In the *New York Times*, a critic complains that the 'the decrepit womanizer' played by the septuagenarian Peter O'Toole in the Hanif Kureishi film *Venus*, and Hector, the elderly teacher 'who gropes his male students' in Alan Bennett's play and film *The History Boys*, are meant to be relatively 'benign', but instead their actual behaviour makes them seem 'venal and self-deluding'. There is what she calls 'a significant ick factor' in watching such elderly people 'stalking' their young victims. But, she argues, instead of portraying these characters as the predators they really are, the filmmakers seem to want us to sympathise with, even applaud, such behaviour. The problem with *The History Boys* is that it 'assumes that the audience will embrace its lecherous hero as fully as the film's creators do'.[28]

In other words, artists should not ask us to try to understand characters we cannot approve of – or not until after they have firmly and unequivocally condemned them. The idea that we might be able to feel that 'ick factor' and simultaneously see life through the eyes of these two ageing and lecherous men, and that this moving out of ourselves into realms beyond our daily experience might be a moral and sympathetic education of its own kind, seems beyond this particular commentator, of whom all one can say is that she is unlikely to be so unforgiving when she herself has reached seventy. But there is nothing egregious about this article. A glance at the thousands of foolish 'reader reviews' on Amazon.com, with their complaints about 'dislikeable characters', confirms a contagion of moralising niceness.

65

On the other side, among those with too little belief in character, we hear that characters do not exist at all. The

[28] Caryn James, 'December and May: Desire vs. Ick Factor', *New York Times*, 15 January 2007.

novelist and critic William Gass comments on the following passage from Henry James's *The Awkward Age*: 'Mr Cashmore, who would have been very red-headed if he had not been very bald, showed a single eyeglass and a long upper lip; he was large and jaunty with little petulant ejaculations that were not in the line of type.' Of this, Gass says:

> We can imagine any number of other sentences about Mr Cashmore added to this one. Now the question is: what is Mr Cashmore? Here is the answer I shall give: Mr Cashmore is (1) a noise, (2) a proper name, (3) a complex system of ideas, (4) a controlling perception, (5) an instrument of verbal organization, (6) a pretended mode of referring, and (7) a source of verbal energy. He is not an object of perception, and nothing whatever that is appropriate to persons can be correctly said of him.[29]

I find this deeply, incorrigibly wrong. Of course characters are assemblages of words, because literature is such an assemblage of words: this tells us absolutely nothing, and is like elaborately informing us that a novel cannot *really* create an imagined 'world', because it is just a bound codex of paper pages. Surely Mr Cashmore, introduced thus by James, has instantly become 'an object of perception' – precisely because we are looking at a description of him. Gass claims that 'nothing whatever that is appropriate to persons can be correctly said of him', but that is exactly what James has just done: he has said of him things that

---

[29] William Gass, *Fiction and the Figures of Life* (1970).

are usually said of a real person. He has told us that Mr Cashmore looked bald and red, and that his 'petulant ejaculations' seemed out of keeping with his large jauntiness ('were not in the line of type'). At present, of course, in James's preliminary dabs, Mr Cashmore has just been created, and he hardly exists; Gass confuses the character's Edenic virginity with his later, Fallen essence. That's to say, Mr Cashmore at this moment is like the frame of one of those buildings we look at from the street, and which so often seem like stage sets. Of course 'any number of other sentences about Mr Cashmore' could be added to the ones we have: that is because so few sentences have so far been said by James about him. The more paint that James applies, the less provisional will the character seem. Gass's words pose as scepticism but in fact simply represent a dandyish flippancy, a refusal to be taught by literature about other people. To my mind, to deny character with such extremity is essentially to deny the novel.

66

But to repeat, what *is* a character? I am thicketed in qualifications: if I say that a character seems connected to consciousness, to the use of a mind, the many superb examples of characters who seem to think very little, who are rarely seen thinking, bristle up (Gatsby, Captain Ahab, Becky Sharpe, Widmerpool, Jean Brodie). If I refine the thought by repeating that a character at least has some essential connection to an interior life, to inwardness, is seen 'from within', I am presented with the nicely opposing examples of those two adulterers, Anna Karenina and Effi Briest, the

82

first of whom does a lot of reflection, and is seen internally as well as externally, the second of whom, in Theodor Fontane's eponymous novel, is seen almost entirely from the outside, with little space set aside for represented reflection. No one could say that Anna is more vivid than Effi simply because we see Anna doing more thinking.

If I try to distinguish between major and minor characters – round and flat characters – and claim that these differ in terms of subtlety, depth, time allowed on the page, I must concede that many so-called flat characters seem more alive to me, and more interesting as human studies, however short-lived, than the round characters they are supposedly subservient to.

67

The novel is the great virtuoso of exceptionalism: it always wriggles out of the rules thrown around it. And the novelistic character is the very Houdini of that exceptionalism. There is no such thing as 'a novelistic character'. There are just thousands of different kinds of people, some round, some flat, some deep, some caricatures, some realistically evoked, some brushed in with the lightest of strokes. Some of them are solid enough that we can speculate about their motives: why does Hurstwood steal the money? Why does Isabel Archer return to Gilbert Osmond? What is Julien Sorel's true ambition? Why does Kirilov want to commit suicide? What does Mr Biswas want? But there are scores of fictional characters who are not fully or conventionally evoked who are also alive and vivid. The solid, nineteenth-century fictional character (I count Biswas in that company) who confronts us with deep mysteries is not the 'best' or ideal or only way to create character (though it does not deserve the enormous condescension of postmodernism). My own taste tends towards the sketchier fictional personage, whose lacunae and omissions tease us, provoke us to wade in their deep shallows: why does Onegin reject Tatiana and then provoke a fight with Lenski? Pushkin offers us almost no evidence on which to base our answer. Is Svevo's Zeno mad? Is the narrator of Hamsun's *Hunger* mad? We have only their unreliable narration of events.

68

Perhaps because I am not sure what a character is, I find especially moving those postmodern novels, like *Pnin*, or *The Prime of Miss Jean Brodie*, or *The Year of the Death of Ricardo Reis*, or Roberto Bolaño's *The Savage Detectives*, in which we are confronted with characters who are at once real and unreal. In all these novels, the author asks us to reflect on the fictionality of the heroes and heroines who give the novels their titles. And in a fine paradox, it is precisely such reflection that stirs in the reader a desire to make these fictional characters 'real', to say, in effect, to the authors: 'I know that they are only fictional – you keep on telling me this. But I can only *know* them by treating them as real.' That is how *Pnin* works, for instance. An unreliable narrator insists that Professor Pnin is 'a character' in two senses of the word: a type (clownish, eccentric émigré), and a fictional character, the narrator's fantasy. Yet precisely because we resent the narrator's condescension towards his fond and foolish posses-sion, we insist that behind the 'type' there must be a real

Pnin, who is worth 'knowing' in all his fullness and complexity. And Nabokov's novel is constructed in such a way as to excite that desire in us for a real Professor Pnin, a 'true fiction' with which to oppose the false fictions of the overbearing and sinister narrator.

69

José Saramago's great novel *The Year of the Death of Ricardo Reis* works a little differently, but to the same effect, and, like *Pnin*, becomes a moving investigation of what a real self is. Ricardo Reis, a doctor from Brazil, is an aloof, conservative aesthete who has decided to return to his native Portugal. It is the end of 1935, and the great poet Fernando Pessoa has just died. Reis is himself a poet and mourns Pessoa's departure. He is not sure what to do. He has saved some money, and for a while he lives in a hotel, where he has an affair with a chambermaid. He writes several beautiful lyrics, and is visited by the now-ghostly Pessoa, with whom he converses. Saramago describes these conversations in a frankly literal and direct manner. Reis wanders the streets of Lisbon, as 1935 curdles into 1936. He reads the newspapers, and is increasingly alarmed by the baying of Europe's dogs: in Spain civil war and the rise of Franco, in Germany Hitler, in Italy Mussolini, and in Portugal the fascist dictatorship of Salazar. He would like to retreat from this bad news. He reflects fondly on the story of the ninety-seven-year-old John D. Rockefeller, who has a specially doctored version of the *New York Times* delivered every day, altered to contain only good news. 'The world's threats are universal, like the sun, but Ricardo Reis takes shelter under his own shadow.'

But Ricardo Reis is not a 'real' fictional character, whatever that means (like David Copperfield or Emma Bovary). He is one of the four pen-names which the actual Pessoa – the poet who worked and lived in Lisbon and died in 1935 – assumed, and in whose persona he wrote poetry. The special flicker of this book, the tint and the delicacy that make it seem hallucinatory, derive from the solidity with which Saramago invests a character who is a fictional character twice over: first Pessoa's, then Saramago's. This enables Saramago to tease us with something that we already know, namely that Ricardo Reis is fictional. Saramago makes something deep and moving of this because Ricardo also feels himself to be somewhat fictional, at best a shadowy spectator, a man on the margin of things. And when Ricardo reflects thus, we feel a strange tenderness for him, aware of something that *he does not know,* that he is not real.

70

Is there a way in which all of us are fictional characters, parented by life and written by ourselves? This is something like Saramago's question; but it is worth noting that he reaches his question by traveling in the opposite direction of those postmodern novelists who like to remind us of the metafictionality of all things. A certain kind of postmodern novelist (like John Barth, say) is always lecturing us: 'Remember, this character is just a character. I invented him.' By starting with an invented character, however, Saramago is able to pass through the same scepticism, but in the opposite direction, toward reality, toward the deepest questions. Saramago asks, in effect: but what *is* 'just a character'? And

Saramago's uncertainty is more real than William Gass's scepticism, for no one ever says, in life, 'I don't exist.' We say, rather, 'I believe I exist,' exactly as Ricardo does.

In Saramago's novels, the self may cast only a shadow, like Ricardo Reis, but this shadow implies not the non-existence of the self, but only its difficult visibility, its near-invisibility, rather as the shadow cast by the sun warns us that we cannot look directly at it. Ricardo Reis is aloof, ghostly. He does not want to get pulled into real relationships, including the real relationships of politics. Europe is scrambling for war, but Ricardo luxuriously sits around wondering if he exists. He writes a poem that begins: 'We count for nothing, we are less than futile.' Another poem begins: 'Walk empty-handed, for wise is the man who contents himself with the spectacle of the world.' Yet the novel suggests that perhaps there is something culpable about being content with the spectacle of the world when the world's spectacle is horrifying.

71

The question of this novel, and of much of Saramago's work, is not the trivial 'metafictional' game-playing of 'Does Ricardo Reis exist?' It is the much more poignant question, 'Do we exist if we refuse to relate to anyone?'

72

What does it mean to 'love' a fictional character, to feel that you know her? What kind of knowledge is this? Miss Jean Brodie is one of the best-loved novelistic characters in postwar British fiction, and one of the very few to be something of a household name. But if you dragged a microphone down Princes Street in Edinburgh and asked people what they 'know' about Miss Brodie, those who had read Muriel Spark's novel would likely recite a number of her aphorisms: 'I am in my prime', 'you are the crème de la crème', 'the philistines are upon us, Mr Lloyd', and so on. These are Jean Brodie's famous sayings. Miss Brodie, in other words, is not really 'known' at all. We know her just as her young pupils knew her: as a collection of tags, a rhetorical performance, a teacher's show. At Marcia Blaine School for girls, each member of the Brodie set is 'famous' for something: Mary Macgregor is famous for being stupid, and Rose is famous for sex, and so on. Miss Brodie, it seems, is famous for her sayings. Around her very thinness as a character we tend to construct a thicker interpretative jacket.

Nearly all of Muriel Spark's novels are fiercely composed and devoutly starved. Her brilliantly reduced style, of 'never apologise, never explain', seems a deliberate provocation: we feel compelled to turn the mere crescents of her characters into solid discs. But while some of her refusal to wax explanatory or sentimental may have been temperamental, it was also moral. Spark was intensely interested in how much we can know about anyone, and interested in how much a novelist, who most pretends to such knowledge, can know about her characters. By reducing Miss Brodie to no more than a collection of maxims, Spark forces *us* to become Brodie's pupils. In the course of the novel we never leave the school to go home with Miss Brodie. We never see her in private, off-stage. Always, she is the performing teacher, keeping a public face. We surmise that there is something unfulfilled and even desperate about her, but the novelist refuses us access to her interior. Brodie talks a great deal about her prime, but we don't witness it, and the nasty suspicion falls that perhaps to talk so much about one's prime is by definition no longer to be in it.

Spark always exercises ruthless control over her fictional characters, and here she flaunts it: she spikes her story with a series of 'flash-forwards' in which we learn what happened to the characters after the main action of the plot (Miss Brodie will die of cancer, Mary Macgregor pupil will die at the age of twenty-three in a fire, another pupil will join a convent, another will have an ordinary marriage, another will never again be quite as happy as when she first discovered algebra). These coldly prophetic passages strike some readers as cruel; they are such summary judgements. But they are moving, because they raise the idea that if Miss Brodie never really had a prime, then for some of the schoolgirls their primes occurred in their childhoods – during those days earnestly praised, at least by one's teachers, as the 'happiest days of your life'.

These flash-forwards do something else: they remind us that Muriel Spark has powers of ultimate control over her creations; and they remind us of . . . Miss Brodie. This tyrannical authority is precisely what Miss Brodie's most intelligent pupil Sandy Stranger[30] hates, and finally exposes, in

---

[30] Sandy *Stranger*: it is astonishing how resilient has been the convention of giving characters allegorical names. But that is because it is not only conventional. There is a real sense in which we are what we are called, at least from the Old Testament onwards, when God renamed Jacob Israel, which means that he struggled with God. Tolstoy, with his usual practicality, wrote an early draft of *War and Peace* in which Count Rostov was simply named Count *Prostoy*: *prostoy* means 'simple, honest' in Russian. So we have Becky Sharpe (in *Vanity Fair*) and Miss Temple (in *Jane Eyre*) and Félicité (in *A Simple Heart*) and scores of characters in Dickens like Crook and Pecksniff, and Charles Ryder and Sebastian

her teacher: that she is a fascist and a Scottish Calvinist, predestining the lives of her pupils, forcing them into artificial shapes. Is this what the novelist does, too? That is the question that interests Spark. The novelist adopts God-like powers of omniscience, but what can she really know of her creations? Surely only God, the ultimate author of our lives, can know our coming and our going, and surely only God has the moral right to decide such things. Nabokov used to say that he pushed his characters around like serfs or chess pieces – he had no time for that metaphorical ignorance and impotence whereby authors like to say, 'I don't know what happened, but my character just got away from me and did his own thing. I had nothing to do with it.'[31] Nonsense, said Nabokov, if I want my character to cross the road, he crosses the road. I am his master. Nabokov's fiction, like Spark's,

---

Flyte in *Brideshead Revisited* (the voyeuristic narrator merely *rides*, while the doomed hero *flees* and then falls), and so on. Fiction is not being very fictional, really, when it resorts to such tricks. After all, in life people do seem uncannily to have become the names they have, or to be the opposite of those names (but still in some strange relation to the import of their names): Wordsworth is surely worth his words, and Kierkegaard means churchyard in Danish, and the late Cardinal Sin was Archbishop of Manila, and a distinguished philosopher called John Wisdom was a student of Wittgenstein's, and one of the current Fellows of Eton College has the highly Waugh-like name of The Hon P. J. Remnant. Shakespeare makes fun of this idea in *Henry IV, Part 1*, when Prince Hal teases Falstaff for cowardice: 'What, a coward, Sir John Paunch?' To which the fat knight replies: 'Indeed, I am not John of Gaunt, your grandfather, but yet no coward, Hal,' to which Muriel Spark wittily replies in *The Prime of Miss Jean Brodie*, when she introduces a nasty schoolmistress 'whose surname was Gaunt and who was in fact gaunt'.

[31] As, by report, Pushkin spoke of Onegin and Tatiana: 'Do you know my Tatiana has rejected my Eugene. I never expected it of her.'

explores the implications of such potency: Timofey Pnin finally refuses to be pushed about by Nabokov's bullying narrator, who seems suspiciously like Nabokov himself. Pnin memorably says that he refuses to 'work under' the narrator (who is coming to head the department where Professor Pnin teaches). This was one of Spark's abiding concerns, from her early novels like *The Comforters* and *Memento Mori*, to her very last, *The Finishing School*. She used fiction to reflect on the responsibilities and limitations of fiction itself, and indeed on the difficulties and limitations of all fiction-making.

73

This fictional self-consciousness, and her devotion to spare forms, made Spark resemble at times a *nouveau romancier* like Alain Robbe-Grillet or the British avant-gardist B. S. Johnson, who once published a novel, *The Unfortunates*, made of looseleaf pages in a box, to be arranged as the reader saw fit. Johnson's slightly more conventional novel, *Christie Malry's Own Double Entry*, is very funny, and studded with amusing metafictional self-consciousness. Christie's mother says things like: 'My son: I have for the purposes of this novel been your mother for the past eighteen years and five months to the day . . .' At his mother's funeral, 'Christie was the only mourner, economy as to relatives (as to so many other things) being one of the virtues of this novel.' Like Nabokov and Spark, B. S. Johnson saw the comparison between God the omniscient author and the omnipotent novelist, who can do anything he likes with his 'chess pieces'. At one point, Christie's mother explains how Adam and Eve first ate from the tree. Of course, she says, the whole thing is absurd, because God could have stopped it any time He liked, being omniscient. 'But no: God has been making it all up as He goes along, like certain kinds of novelist . . .'

But the difference between Johnson and Spark is instructive, too. Johnson plays with these questions but does not finally *inhabit* them as Spark or Nabokov or Saramago do. In the end there is nothing like the pressure of enquiry you feel in those writers. Johnson is content to ask, again and again – and very entertainingly – the metafictional question 'Does Christie exist?' but not the metaphysical question 'How does Christie exist?' – which is really the question 'How do *we* exist?' The reason for the atmosphere of postmodern lightness in this novel is that Johnson is not able to be gravely sceptical because he is not able to be gravely affirmative (the opposite of Saramago, as we saw, who wrings scepticism out of affirmation). Jean Brodie, though we see her in only a handful of scenes that are shuffled like a pack of cards, *exists* for Spark, has metaphysical presence, and does for us, too. That is why the questions 'Who was Jean Brodie? Who really knew her?' have power and affect. But Christie Malry does not really exist for Johnson. He is denied before he is believed in. [32]

---

[32] Philip Roth's *The Counterlife* is an example of another novel that takes what it needs from metafictional game-playing to make a grave and fundamentally metaphysical argument about the different ways of living, and narrating, a life. Gabriel Josipovici discusses Beckett in this spirit in his book *On Trust* (2000). He points out that Foucault liked to quote from *The Unnamable*, as evidence of the death of the author: 'No matter who is speaking, someone says, no matter who is speaking,' wrote Beckett. Josipovici comments that Foucault forgets that 'it is not Beckett saying this but one of his characters, and that the point about that character is that he is desperately seeking to discover *who* speaks, to recover himself as more than a string of words, to wrest an "I" from "someone says".'

To argue that we can know Jean Brodie just as deeply as we can know Dorothea Brooke, to argue that lacunae are as deep as solidities, that absence in characterisation can be a form of knowing as profound as presence, that Spark's and Saramago's and Nabokov's characters can move us as much as James's and Eliot's, is to concede nothing to William Gass's scepticism. Not all of these characters have the same amount of realised 'depth', but all of them are objects of perception, to use Gass's words, all of them are more than mere bundles of words (though of course they *are* bundles of words), and things that can be correctly said of persons can also be said of them. They are all 'real' (they have a reality) but in different ways. That reality-level differs from author to author, and our hunger for the particular depth or reality-level of a character is tutored by each writer, and adapts to the internal conventions of each book. This is how we can read W. G. Sebald one day, and Woolf the next, and Philip Roth the next, and not demand that each resemble the other. It would be an obvious category mistake to accuse Sebald of not offering us 'deep' or 'rounded' characters, or to accuse Woolf of not offering us plenty of juicy, robust minor characters in the way of Dickens. I think that novels tend to fail not when the characters are not vivid or deep enough, but when the novel in question has failed to teach us how to adapt to its conventions, has failed to manage a specific hunger for its own characters, its own reality-level. In such cases, our appetite is quickly disappointed, and surges wildly in excess of what we are provided, and we tend to blame the author for not giving us enough – the characters, we complain, are not alive or round or free enough. Yet we would not dream of accusing Sebald or Woolf or Roth – none of whom is especially interested in creating character in the solid, old-fashioned nineteenth-century sense – of letting us down in this way, because they have so finely tutored us in their own conventions, their own expansive limitations, to be satisfied with just what they give us.

75

Even the characters we think of as 'solidly realised' in the conventional realist sense, are less solid the longer we look at them. I think there is a basic distinction to be made between novelists like Tolstoy or Trollope or Balzac or Dickens, or dramatists like Shakespeare, who are rich in 'negative capability', who seem unselfconsciously to create galleries of various people who are nothing like them, and those writers either less interested in, or perhaps less naturally gifted at, this faculty, but who nevertheless have a great deal of interest in the self – James, Flaubert, Lawrence, Woolf perhaps, Musil, Bellow, Michel Houellebecq, Philip Roth. Bellow's vibrating individuals are Dickensianly vivid, and Bellow himself was aesthetically and philosophically interested in the individual , but no one would call him a great creator of fictional individuals. We don't go around saying to ourselves 'what would Augie March or Charlie Citrine do?'[33] Iris Murdoch is the most poignant member of this second category, precisely because she spent her life trying

---

[33] Except the hero and narrator of Frederick Exley's one good novel, *A Fan's Notes*, who explicitly invokes the example of Augie.

to get into the first. In her literary and philosophical criticism, she again and again stresses that the creation of free and independent characters is the mark of the great novelist; yet her own characters never have this freedom. She knew it, too: 'How soon one discovers that, however much one is in the ordinary sense "interested in other people," this interest has left one far short of possessing the knowledge required to create a character who is not oneself. It is impossible, it seems to me, not to see one's failure here as a sort of spiritual failure.'[34]

76

But Murdoch is too unforgiving of herself. There are scores of novelists whose characters are basically like each other, or rather like the novelist who created them, and yet whose creations stream with a vitality that it would be hard not to call free. Does *The Rainbow* possess any characters who don't sound like each other, and ultimately like D. H. Lawrence? Tom Brangwen, Will, Anna, Ursula, even Lydia – they are all variations on a Lawrencian theme, and despite differences in articulacy and education, their inner lives vibrate very similarly. When they speak, which is rarely, they sound the same. Nevertheless, they do possess blazing inner lives, and always one feels how important this enquiry into the state of the soul is for the novelist himself. In some sense, the scenes – the battles of husband and wife, of two opposed and proximate egos – are more individuated than the

---

[34] Murdoch, 'The Sublime and the Beautiful Revisited', in *Existentialists and Mystics: Writings on Philosophy and Literature* (1997).

characters themselves: Will and Anna stacking sheaves of corn in the harvest moonlight; the chapter called 'Anna Victrix', which describes the first, swooning months of the marriage, as Will and Anna discover the sublimity of their sexual union and realise that the world is insignificant to the passion they share; pregnant Anna dancing naked in her bedroom, as David once danced before the Lord, while Will looks on enviously; the chapter devoted to the visit to Lincoln Cathedral; the great flood, which kills Tom Brangwen; Ursula and Skrebensky, kissing under the moon; Ursula at the oppressive school in Ilkeston; Skrebensky and Ursula running away to London and Paris – in a London hotel room she watches him bathing: 'He was slender, and, to her, perfect, a clean, straight-cut youth, without a grain of superfluous body.'

In the same way, it often seems that James's characters are not especially convincing as independently vivid authorial creations. But what makes them vivid is the force of James's interest in them, his manner of pressing into their clay with his examining fingers: they are sites of human energy; they vibrate with James's anxious concern for them. Take *The Portrait of a Lady*. It is very hard to say what Isabel Archer is *like*, exactly, and she seems to lack the definition, the depth if you like, of a heroine like Dorothea Brooke, in *Middlemarch*.

I think this was deliberate on James's part. His novel begins with extraordinary stiffness and self-consciousness: three men, engaged in frivolous badinage, are sitting having tea, waiting for the arrival of the host's niece. They talk about this lady. Isn't she due soon? Will she be pretty? Perhaps one of the men will marry her? And then at the very start of the second chapter, she obligingly arrives. Were

James being 'workshopped' in a creative writing course, he would be censured for this speedy awkwardness; he should surely put a chapter of naturalistic filler between the men at tea and the arrival, make it look a bit less novelistic and convenient. But James's point is that these men – and by extension we the readers – are waiting for the arrival of a *heroine*; and, sure enough, here is the author stepping up to provide her. James then proceeds, over the next forty or so pages, to hand us an enormous plate of commentary about Isabel, much of it contradictory. It is presented to us by the author in full exegetical mode. Isabel is brilliant, but perhaps only by the standards of provincial Albany; Isabel wants freedom, but really she is afraid of it; Isabel wants to suffer, but really she doesn't believe in suffering; she is egotistical, but she likes nothing better than to humble herself, and so on. It is essentially a mess of propositions, and there is very little attempt to present Isabel dramatically. It is an essay, an essay on a character. And it is mostly James telling and not showing.

77

James is really suggesting that he has not yet formed his character, that she is still relatively shapeless, an American emptiness, and that the *novel* will form her, for good and ill, that Europe will fill in her shape, and that just as these three waiting, watching men will also form her, so will we, as readers. They and we are a kind of Greek chorus, hanging on her every move. Two of the men, Lord Warburton and Ralph Touchett, will devote their lives to watching her. And what, James asks, will be the plot that poor Isabel will have written for her? How much will she herself write it, and how much will be written for her by others? And in the end, will we really know what Isabel was like, or will we have merely painted a portrait of a lady?

So the vitality of literary character has less to do with dramatic action, novelistic coherence and even plain plausibility – let alone likeability – than with a larger, philosophical or metaphysical sense, our awareness that a character's actions are profoundly *important*, that something profound is at stake, with the author brooding over the face of that character like God over the face of the waters. That is how readers retain in their minds a sense of the character 'Isabel Archer', even if they cannot tell you what she is exactly like. We remember her in the way we remember an obscurely significant day: something important has been enacted here.

78

In *Aspects of the Novel*, Forster used the now-famous term 'flat' to describe the kind of character who is awarded a single, essential attribute, which is repeated without change as the person appears and reappears in a novel. Often, such characters have a catchphrase or tagline or keyword, as Mrs Micawber, in *David Copperfield*, likes to repeat 'I will never desert Mr Micawber.' She says she will not, and she does not. Forster is genially snobbish about flat characters, and wants to demote them, reserving the highest category for rounder, or fuller characters. Flat characters cannot be tragic, he asserts, they need to be comic. Round characters 'surprise' us each time they reappear; they are not flimsily theatrical; they combine well with other characters in conversation, 'and draw one another out without seeming to do so'. Flat ones can't surprise us, and are generally monochromatically histrionic. Forster mentions a popular novel by a contemporary novelist whose main character, a flat one, is a farmer who is always saying 'I'll plough up that bit of gorse.' But, says Forster, we are so bored by the farmer's consistency that we do not care whether he does or doesn't. Mrs Micawber, he suggests, has a saving comic lightness, which allows her to be similarly consistent but not similarly dull.

But is this right? Of course, we know a caricature when we see one, and caricature is generally uninteresting. (Though sometimes it might just be a novelist's way of sticking to the point . . .) But if by flatness we mean a character, often but not always a minor one, often but not always comic, who serves to illuminate an essential human truth or characteristic, then many of the most interesting characters are flat. I would be quite happy to abolish the very idea of 'roundness' in characterisation, because it tyrannises us – readers, novelists, critics – with an impossible ideal. 'Roundness' is impossible in fiction, because fictional characters, while very alive in their way, are not the same as real people (though, of course, there are many real people, in real life, who are quite flat and don't seem very round – which I will come to). It is subtlety that matters – subtlety of analysis, of inquiry, of concern, of felt pressure – and for subtlety a very small point of entry will do. Forster's division grandly privileges novels over short stories, since characters in stories rarely have the space to become 'round'. But I learn more about the consciousness of the soldier in Chekhov's *The Kiss* than I do about the consciousness of Becky Sharpe in *Vanity Fair*, because Chekhov's inquiry into how his soldier's mind works is more acute than Thackeray's serial vividness. [35]

In the second place, many of the most vivid characters in fiction are monomaniacs. There is Hardy's Michael Henchard, in *The Mayor of Casterbridge*, who burns with his one secret, or Gould in *Nostromo*, who can think only of his mine. Casaubon, too, fixated on his infinite book. Aren't such people essentially flat? They may surprise us at first, but they soon stop surprising us, as their central need occu-

---

[35] Spatial metaphors, of depth, shallowness, roundness, flatness, are inadequate. A better division – though not perfect either – is between transparencies (relatively simple characters) and opacities (relative degrees of mysteriousness). Many of the most absorbing accounts of motive, from Hamlet to Stavrogin to the subjects of W. G. Sebald's *The Emigrants*, are studies in mystery. Stephen Greenblatt argues in *Will in The World: How Shakespeare Became Shakespeare* (2004) that in his tragedies, Shakespeare systematically reduced the amount of 'causal explanation a tragic plot needed to function effectively and the amount of explicit psychological rationale a character needed to be compelling. Shakespeare found that he could immeasurably deepen the effect of his plays, that he could provoke in the audience and in himself a peculiarly passionate intensity of response, if he took out a key explanatory element, thereby occluding the rationale, motivation, or ethical principle that accounted for the action that was to unfold. The principle was not the making of a riddle to be solved, but the creation of a strategic opacity.' Why does Lear test his daughters? Why can't Hamlet effectively avenge the death of his father? Why does Iago ruin Othello's life? The source texts that Shakespeare read all provided transparent answers (Iago was in love with Desdemona, Hamlet should kill Claudius, Lear was unhappy with Cordelia's impending marriage). But Shakespeare was not interested in such transparency. Greenblatt's argument also touches on paragraph 87, where I show how the novel threw off the essential juvenility of plot in favour of 'unconsummated stories', and paragraph 97, where I discuss the novel's possible contribution to Bernard Williams's desire for complexity in moral philosophy.

pies them. Yet they are no less vivid, interesting, or true as creations, for being flat. They are certainly not cartoons, which is implicit in Forster's discussion. (They are not cartoons because their monomania is not inherently cartoonish but inherently interesting – *consistently surprising*, one might say.)

Forster struggles to explain how we feel that most of Dickens's characters are flat and yet at the same time that these cameos obscurely move us – he claims that Dickens's own vitality makes them 'vibrate' a bit on the page. But this vibrating flatness is true not only of Dickens, but of Proust, who also likes to tag many of his characters with favourite sayings and catchphrases, of Tolstoy to some extent, of Hardy's minor characters, of Mann's minor characters (he, like Proust and Tolstoy, uses a method of mnemonic leitmotif – a repeated attribute or characteristic – to secure the vitality of his characters), and supremely of Jane Austen.

79

Forster mysteriously claims Austen for the round-character camp, but in doing so he just shows that he needs to expand his definition of flatness. For what is striking about Austen is precisely that only her heroines are really capable of development and surprise: they are the only characters who possess consciousness, the only characters who are seen thinking in any depth, and they are heroic, in part, *because* they possess the secret of consciousness. The minor characters around them, by contrast, are pretty obviously flat. They are seen externally, they revel themselves only in speech, and little is demanded of them: Mr Collins, Miss Bates, Mr Woodhouse,

101

and so on. The minor characters belong to a certain stage of theatrical satire; the heroines belong to the newly emergent, newly complex form of the novel.

Take Shakespeare's *Henry V* as an example. If you asked most people to separate King Harry and the Welsh captain Fluellen into Forsterian camps, they would award Harry roundness and Fluellen flatness. The King is a large part, Fluellen a minor one. Harry talks and reflects a lot, he soliloquises, he is noble, canny, magniloquent, and surprising: he goes among his soldiers in disguise, to talk freely with them. He complains of the burden of kingship. Fluellen, by contrast, is a comic Welshman, a pedant of the kind Fielding or Cervantes would nimbly satirise, always banging on about military history, and Alexander the Great, and leeks, and Monmouth. Harry rarely makes us laugh, Fluellen always does. Harry is round, Fluellen flat. Which actor, at audition, would choose Fluellen over the part of the King? ('I'm sorry, sir, Mr Branagh has already reserved that part for himself.')

But the categories could easily go the other way. The King Harry of this play, unlike the Harry of the two *Henry IV* plays, is merely kingly, in rather a dull fashion. He is very eloquent, but it seems like Shakespeare's eloquence, not his own (it's formal, patriotic, august). His complaints about the burdens of kingship are a bit formulaic and self-pitying, and tell us little about his actual self (except, in a generic way, that he is self-pitying). He is an utterly public figure. Fluellen, by contrast, is a little terrier of vividness. His speech, despite the 'Welshisms' that Shakespeare puts in – 'look you', and so on – is idiosyncratically his own. He is a pedant, but an interesting one. In Fielding, a pedantic doctor or lawyer speaks like a pedantic doctor or lawyer: his pedantry is professionally bound up with his occupation. But Fluellen's pedantry has a limitless, and slightly desperate quality about it: why does he know so much about the classics, about Alexander the Great and Philip of Macedon? Why has he appointed himself the army's military historian? He surprises us, too: at first we think his windiness will substitute for valour on the field, as Falstaff's did, because we think we recognise a type – the man who speaks about military action rather than performing it. But he turns out to possess a touching valour and loyalty; and his rectitude – another inversion of type – is not merely hypocritical. (That is, he does not *just* talk about rectitude, even though he does indeed talk a lot about it.) And there is something piquant about a man who is at once an omnivorous roamer of the world's knowledge and literatures, and at the same time a little Welsh provincial. His monologue on how Monmouth resembles the classical city of Macedon is both funny and moving:

> I tell you, captain, if you look in the maps of the worlds
> I warrant you shall find, in the comparisons between
> Macedon and Monmouth, that the situations, look you,
> is both alike. There is a river in Macedon, and there is
> also moreover a river in Monmouth.

I still meet people like Fluellen; and when a garrulous guy on a train starts talking up his home town, and says something like 'we've got one of those' – shopping mall, opera house, violent pub – 'in my town, too, you know,' you are apt to feel, as towards Fluellen, both mirth and an obscure kind of sympathy, since this kind of importuning provincialism is always paradoxical: the provincial simultaneously wants and does not want to communicate with you, simultaneously wants to remain a provincial and abolish his provincialism by linking himself with you. Almost four hundred years later, in a story called 'The Wheelbarrow', V. S. Pritchett revisits Fluellen. A Welsh taxi-driver, Evans, is helping a lady clear out a house. He finds an old volume of verse in a box, and suddenly bursts out, scornfully: 'Everyone knows that the Welsh are the founders of all the poetry in Europe.'

80

In fact, the ubiquitous flat character of the English novel, from Mr Collins to Charles Ryder's father, tells us something deep about the dialectic of British reticence and sociability, and something, too, about British theatricality. It is hardly surprising that the self should be so often theatrical in English fiction, when its great progenitor is Shakespeare. But of course many of Shakespeare's characters are not just theatrical; they are self-theatricalising. They carry within them fantastic, often illusory, notions of their own prowess and reputation. This is true of Lear, of Antony, of Cleopatra, of Richard II, of Falstaff, of Othello (who, as he is dying, is still instructing his audience to make a record of his demise: 'Set you down this,/ And say besides that in Aleppo once . . . I took by th' throat the circumcised dog/ And smote him thus'). And it is true, too, of the minor characters like Launce and Bottom and Mistress Quickly, who so easily flame up into histrionic comic irrelevance.

From Shakespeare descends a self-theatricalising, somewhat solipsistic, flamboyant, but also perhaps essentially shy type who can be found in Fielding, Austen, Dickens, Hardy, Thackeray, Meredith, Wells, Henry Green, Evelyn Waugh,

V. S. Pritchett, Muriel Spark, Angus Wilson, Martin Amis, Zadie Smith, and on into the superb pantomimic embarrassments of Monty Python and Ricky Gervais's David Brent. He is typified by Mr Omer, in *David Copperfield*, the tailor whom David visits to get his funeral suit. (David is en route to his mother's funeral.) Mr Omer is an English soliloquist, and prattles on without embarrassment as he blunders his way all over David's grief: 'after showing me a roll of cloth which he said was extra super, and too good mourning for anything short of parents . . . "But fashions are like human beings. They come in, nobody knows when, why or how; and they go out, nobody knows when, why, or how. Everything is like life, in my opinion, if you look at it in that point of view."'

Something true is revealed here about the self and its irrepressibility or irresponsibility – the little riot of freedom in otherwise orderly souls, the self's chink of freedom, its gratuity or surplus, its tip to itself. Mr Omer is determined to *be himself*, even if that means likening fashions in clothes to patterns of morbidity. Yet no one would call Mr Omer a 'round' character. He exists for a bare minute. But *contra* Forster, the flat character like Mr Omer is indeed capable of 'surprising us' – the point is, *he only needs to surprise us once*, and can then disappear off the stage.

Mrs Micawber's catchphrase 'I will never desert Mr Micawber' tells us something true about how she keeps up appearances, how she maintains a theatrical public fiction, and so it tells us something true about *her*; but the farmer who says 'I'll plough up that bit of gorse' is not maintaining any similarly interesting fiction about himself – he is just being stoical or habitual – and so we know nothing about his true self behind the catchphrase. He is simply stating his agronomic intentions. That is why he is boring; 'consistency' has nothing to do with it. And we all know people in real life who, like Mrs Micawber, do indeed use a series of jingles and tags and repetitive gestures to maintain a certain kind of performance.

A BRIEF HISTORY OF
CONSCIOUSNESS

81

One reason that Cervantes needs to have Don Quixote accompanied by Sancho Panza on his travels is that the Knight must have someone to talk to. When Don Quixote sends Sancho off to search for Dulcinea, and is alone for the first extended period in the novel, he does not *think*, as we would now understand the term. He speaks out aloud, he soliloquises.

The novel begins in the theatre, and novelistic characterisation begins when the soliloquy goes inward. The soliloquy, in turn, has its origins in prayer, as we can see from Greek tragedy, or from Book 5 of *The Odyssey*, or from the Psalms, or from David's songs to the Lord in 1 and 2 Samuel. Shakespeare's heroes and heroines still use soliloquy to invoke the Gods, if not quite to pray to them: 'Come you spirits . . . unsex me here', 'Blow winds and crack your cheeks', and so on. The actor comes to the front of the stage and speaks his mind to an audience, who is both God above and we spectators in the seats. Nineteenth-century novelists like Charlotte Brontë and Thomas Hardy continued to describe their characters as 'soliloquising' when speaking to themselves.

The novel has changed the art of characterisation partly by changing *who a character is being seen by*. Consider three men, each permanently affected by a chance occurrence: King David in the Old Testament; Macbeth; and Raskolnikov in *Crime and Punishment*. David, strolling on his roof, sees Bathsheba, naked, sunning herself, and is instantly struck with lust. His decision to take her as his lover and wife, and to kill her inconvenient husband, sets in train a series of events that will lead to his downfall and his punishment by God. Macbeth is instantly contaminated by the suggestion of the three witches that he kill the King and take his mantle. He too, is punished – if not explicitly by God, then by 'even-handed justice', and by 'pity, like a naked newborn babe'. And Raskolnikov, in a story clearly influenced by Shakespeare's play, is similarly polluted by an idea – that by killing a miserable pawnbroker, he can vault himself over ordinary morality like a Napoleon. He, too, must 'accept his punishment' as Dostoevsky puts it, and be corrected by God.

82

Despite the many revelations and subtleties of the Old Testament narrative – David's political canniness, his sorrow at the way Saul treats him, his lust for Bathsheba, his grief at the death of his son, Absalom – David remains a public character. In the modern sense, he has no privacy. He hardly ever speaks his inner thoughts to himself; he speaks to God, and his soliloquies are prayers. He is external to us because in some way he *does not exist for us*, but for the Lord. He is seen by the Lord, is transparent to the Lord, but remains opaque to us. This opacity allows for a lovely margin of surprise, to use E. M. Forster's word. For instance, David is cursed by God, who tells him, through the offices of Nathan the prophet, that the house of David will be punished, beginning with his son. And indeed, David's son dies soon after birth. David's response is curious. While the child is ill, he fasts and weeps, but as soon as the child has died he washes, changes his clothes, worships God, and asks his servants to put out food. When they ask him why he has acted thus, he replies: 'While the child was still alive I fasted and wept, for I thought, "Who knows, the LORD may favor me and the child will live." And now that he is dead, why should I fast? Can I bring him back again? I am going to him and he will not come back to me.' (2 Samuel 12:23) Robert Alter, whose modern English translation this is, comments: 'David here acts in a way that neither his courtiers nor the audience of the story could have anticipated.'

David's calm, massive resignation ('I am going to him and he will not come back to me') is beautiful, as well as surprising. David is 'light in spirit'. Despite God's curse, despite the loss of this son, and of Absalom, David dies in his bed, telling his son Solomon that 'I go the way of all the earth.'

David is opaque to us, one feels, precisely because he is transparent to God, who is his real audience. What matters to the Bible-writer is not the state of David's mind, but the whole story, the entirety of the arc of David's life. And this story, this arc, is both human and not quite human – not quite, because causation is divine as well as human. David's life is determined partly by what he does, but the rest of his life is then over-determined, one might say, by God's punishment of him. In a sense, the storyteller is God, who is writing fate's script. David does not have a mind, as we understand modern subjectivity. He has no past, to speak of, and no memory, for it is God's memory that counts, which never forgets. And when he sees Bathsheba, what happens to him is not an idea, or at least not in the way that Jesus, that cheerless psychologist, meant when he said that for a man to look lustfully upon a woman is already to commit adultery. Jesus here announces that mental states are as important as actions. But for the writer of the David story, the mental state is precisely what is occluded; action is all: 'and he saw from the roof a woman bathing, and the woman was very beautiful. And David sent and inquired after the woman, and the one he sent said, "Why, this is Bathsheba daughter of Eliam, wife of Uriah the Hittite." And David sent messengers and fetched her and she came to him and he lay with her, she having just cleansed herself of her impurity, and she returned to her house. And the woman became pregnant . . .' David sees, and acts. As far as the narrative is concerned, he does not think.

83

Macbeth is not being seen by God so much as he is being seen by us, the audience. His prayers, you might say, are soliloquies, and get very close to mental thought, as he agonises before us over the dilemma he finds himself in. One reason for the play's power has to do with its domestic intimacy, whereby we feel we are eavesdropping on the horrid privacy of the Macbeths' marriage, not to mention the guilt-tainted outpourings of their monologues. At certain moments, the play seems to want to pull away and develop itself into a new form, the form of the novel. At the banquet, for instance, in III:4, when Macbeth sees Banquo's ghost,

Lady Macbeth twice leans over to him and attempts to strengthen his resolve. We have to imagine the characters almost whispering to each other in the presence of their guests. 'What, quite unmanned in folly?' says Lady Macbeth. 'If I stand here, I saw him,' replies Macbeth. 'Fie, for shame!' is the fierce spousal response. This is always awkward when acted on stage, because the attendant lords must murmur in the background – in an unconvincing, stagey way – as if they cannot hear what is being said. The privacy of the marital conversation is what poses a theatrical difficulty: where, on stage, can it realistically happen? I think Shakespeare is essentially being a novelist at such moments. On the page, of course, such moments have as much space to exist as the novelist feels like awarding; it is a simple matter of the adjustment of point of view ('Lady Macbeth turned quickly to her blanched Lord, gripped his hand with sharp nails, and hissed at him, "What, quite unmanned in folly?"')

David's story is almost entirely public; Macbeth's is one of publicised privacy. And this private man differs from David in being the possessor of a memory. It is the memory – 'the warder of the brain' – that will not leave Macbeth alone. 'My dull brain was wrought/ With things forgotten,' says Macbeth, pathetically, but the play in fact bodies forth De Quincey's terrifying, pre-Freudian admonition in his *Confessions of an English Opium-Eater*: 'There is no such thing as forgetting.' So the real curse on the Macbeths is not theological, despite the machinery of the witches, and the ghosts; the real curse is mental, 'the written troubles of the brain'. Now a character's thought can be *retrospective*, can move back and forth over the present and the past, to take in a whole life:

I have lived long enough. My way of life
Is fall'n into the sere, the yellow leaf,
And that which should accompany old age,
As honour, love obedience, troops of friends,
I must not look to have . . .

84

If Macbeth's story is one of publicised privacy, Raskolnikov's
story is one of scrutinised privacy. God still exists, but he is
not watching Raskolnikov – at least, not until the end of
the novel, when Raskolnikov accepts Christ. Until that
moment, Raskolnikov is being watched by us, the readers.
The crucial difference between this and the theatre is that
we are invisible. In David's story the audience is in some
important way irrelevant; in Macbeth's the audience is visible
and silent, and soliloquy does indeed have the feeling not
only of an address to an audience but a conversation with
an interlocutor – us – who will not respond, a blocked
dialogue; in Raskolnikov's story the audience – the reader –
is invisible but all-seeing; so the reader has replaced David's
God and Macbeth's audience.

85

What are the implications of this enormous shift? The
obvious one is that soliloquy does not have to be voiced,
and can get closer to being true mental speech. The hero is
released from the tyranny of necessary eloquence; he is an
ordinary man. (This is just what Raskolnikov cannot bear.)
Inner soliloquy can indulge in repetition, ellipsis, hysteria,

vagueness – mental stutter. If Shakespeare's characters often seem to be overhearing themselves when they soliloquise,[36] *we* are now overhearing Raskolnikov. There is no facet of his soul not tilted toward us. Something else worth noticing is that while David has no mind, to speak of, and Macbeth's mind is punished, Raskolnikov's mind is the author of its own woe; the idea of murdering the woman was his free invention.

Under the new dispensation of the invisible audience, the novel becomes the great analyst of unconscious motive, since the character is released from having to voice his motives: the reader becomes the hermeneut, looking between the lines for the *actual* motive. On the other hand, the absence of a visible audience seems to make the ordinary man *seek* an audience, in ways that would have seemed grotesque to lordly figures like the Macbeths. Many of the characters in *Crime and Punishment* seem compelled to act out horrid pantomimes and melodramas, in which they stage a version of themselves, for effect. David and Macbeth were men of action – you might say they were naturally dramatic (they knew who their audiences were); Raskolnikov is unnaturally theatrical, or better still, histrionic: he seeks attention, and he is desperately unstable and inauthentic, hiding at one moment, confessing at another, proud in one scene, self-abasing in the next. In the novel, we can see the self better than any literary form has yet allowed; but it is not going too far to say that the self is driven mad by being so invisibly scrutinised.

---

[36] This is Harold Bloom's formulation, in *The Western Canon* (1994) and elsewhere.

The novel has shown a stunning technical progression in its ability to render plot, and in making us attend to psychological motivation. In his essay 'The End of the Novel', Osip Mandelstam claimed that 'the novel was perfected and strengthened over an extremely long period of time as the art form to interest the reader in the fate of the individual', singling out two technical refinements: (1) the transformation of biography (the Saint's Life, the moralising Theophrastan sketch and so on) into a meaningful narrative or plot, and (2) 'psychological motivation'.

87

Adam Smith, in his *Lectures on Rhetoric and Belles Lettres*, complains of the relatively young form of the novel that 'as newness is the only merit in a Novel and curiosity the only motive which induces us to read them, the writers are necessitated to make use of this method [i.e. Suspense] to keep it up'. This is an early, mid-eighteenth-century attack on the mindlessness of suspense – the kind of complaint nowadays made routinely about thrillers and pulp fiction.

But the novel soon showed itself willing to surrender the essential juvenility of plot, in favour of what Viktor Shklovsky calls 'unconsummated' stories with 'false endings' (he was referring to Flaubert and Chekhov, respectively).[37] To return to the case of Iris Murdoch, who so wanted to create free characters and so often failed, her failure is not one of psychological attention or metaphysical shallowness – quite the

---

[37] In Shklovsky, *Theory of Prose* (trans. Benjamin Sher, 1990).

opposite – but a Fielding-like devotion to excessive plot-making. Her improbable, melodramatic, feeble stories, still highly indebted to eighteenth- and nineteenth-century theatrics, are not adult enough to take the strain of her complex moral analysis.[38]

88

As Mandelstam wrote, the novel probably has its origins in a secular response to the religious lives and biographies of saints and holy men, and in the tradition inaugurated by the Greek writer Theophrastus, who offered a series of sketches of types – the miser, the hypocrite, the fond and foolish lover, and so on. (*Don Quixote* belongs to the modern novel in part because Cervantes is so determined to discredit

---

[38] To my mind, this is also a weakness with a certain kind of postmodern novel – say, Thomas Pynchon's *Against the Day* – still in love with the rapid, farce-like, overlit simplicities of Fielding. There is nothing more eighteenth-century than Pynchon's love of picaresque plot-accumulation, his mockery of pedantry which is at the same time a love of pedantry, his habit of making his flat characters dance for a moment on stage and then whisking them away, his vaudevillian fondness for silly names, japes, mishaps, disguises, farcical errors, and so on. There are pleasures to be had from these amiable, peopled canvases, and there are passages of great beauty, but, as in farce, the cost to final seriousness is considerable: everyone is ultimately protected from real menace because no one really exists. The massive turbines of the incessant story-making make so much noise that no one can be heard. The Nazi Captain Blicero in *Gravity's Rainbow*, or the ruthless financier Scarsdale Vibe in *Against the Day*, are not truly frightening figures, because they are not true figures. But Gilbert Osmond, Herr Naphta, Peter Verkhovensky and Conrad's anarchist professor are very frightening indeed.

the 'holy' chivalric tales of Arthur and Amadis of Gaul.) Since these were discrete portraits, you could not contrast one with the other.

The Theophrastan and religious tendency remained strong in the novel throughout the eighteenth and nineteenth centuries, and is still visible in cinema and in various kinds of pulp fiction: villains are villains, heroes are heroes, and the good and the bad are clearly separated and delineated – think of Fielding, Goldsmith, Scott, Dickens, Waugh. Character is essentially stable, has fixed attributes, in such writers.

But at the same time, another kind of novel was developing, in which good and bad wars within a single character, and the self refuses to stay still. What the novel powerfully began to do was to explore characterological relativity. This tradition in turn would influence the English and American novel in the early decades of the twentieth century, particularly as Dostoevsky began to be translated into English (Lawrence, Conrad, Ford and Woolf were the chief beneficiaries). And all this can be traced pretty much to one extraordinary novel, *Rameau's Nephew*, written by Denis Diderot in the 1760s, though not published until 1784. In this furious dialogue (it is laid out on the page like a play) an obscure nephew of the famous composer J.-P. Rameau engages in a fictional encounter with an interlocutor named 'Diderot'. Rameau's nephew seems, at first, a recognisable enough French type – a sophisticated cynic, a man who sees through society, a Juvenal of the Luxembourg Gardens. But Diderot's brilliant addition is to complicate this figure by making him resentfully dependent on his famous uncle, the composer. Rameau's nephew plays party tricks like mimicking his uncle's music, which he says he finds boring, by sitting at a fake piano, playing fake music, all the while grimacing and sweating and crooning. He is very unstable; he is described by Diderot as someone who changes from month to month. There is a hollowness, too, because he wants to be famous: 'I would like to be somebody else, at the risk of being a man of genius, a great man . . . Yes, yes, I am mediocre and angry.' He says that he has never listened to his uncle's music without ruefully thinking, 'That's what you will never do.' He dilates on his envy: 'I who have composed keyboard pieces which nobody plays, but which may well be the only ones to go down to future generations who will.' He admires the criminal's daring alienation from society, as Raskolnikov will do.

Where his interlocutor – the Diderot figure – sees reason and order in society, Rameau sees only hypocrisy. The Diderot figure says that he constantly reads 'La Bruyère, Molière, and Theophrastus' – the didactic creators of stable, moralising, satiric characterisation. He says that such writers teach knowledge of one's duties, love of virtue, hatred of vice, which is exactly what we would expect him pompously to say. Rameau's nephew replies that all he has learned from these writers is the value of fraudulence and hypocrisy: 'When I read *Tartuffe* I tell myself: "be a hypocrite, by all means, but don't talk like one. Keep the vices that come in useful to you, but don't have either the tone or the appearance, which would expose you to ridicule."' (Through this conversation, Diderot makes his comment on the kind of simpler characterisation that his own book has outstripped.) Rameau's nephew is a jester, a Fool, but the richness of the book lies in its subtle suggestions that he may be a kind of frustrated genius, possibly more talented than his uncle.

From this character flows some of the psychological flamboyance and acuity of Stendhal, Dostoevsky, Hamsun,

Conrad, Italo Svevo, Ralph Ellison's *Invisible Man*, and *Wittgenstein's Nephew*, in which Thomas Bernhard, following Diderot, raises the possibility that Paul Wittgenstein, the famous philosopher's nephew, was a greater philosopher than his uncle precisely because he did not write his philosophy down.

89

Look at what Stendhal does with this inheritance in *The Red and the Black*, published in 1830: Julien Sorel is strikingly unpredictable. Like Diderot's Rameau, Julien seethes with satiric callousness, self-interested impropriety and gratuitous resentments. He is determined to make Madame de Renal love him not out of any natural impulse but in the proud belief that this is how to conquer society, and how to repay the slights he feels she has given him: 'Julien said to himself, What do I know of this woman's character? Only this – before I went away, I took hold of her hand and she withdrew it; today I withdraw my hand and she takes hold of it and presses it. There's a fine opportunity of paying her back all the contempt she has felt for me. Heaven knows how many lovers she's had. Possibly she only decided to favour me because it's so easy for us to meet.'[39]

Stendhal's superb addition to this complex creature is

---

[39] And it is no accident that this leap forwards in characterisation is accompanied by great technical developments: Stendhal's loose, relaxed, chatty kind of writing allows him to write a kind of interior monologue which is very close to stream-of-consciousness; one passage of this kind of narration, fairly late in the novel, continues for four pages without interruption.

subtly to reveal that, whatever he may say to himself, Julien is actually, unconsciously, in love with Madame de Renal. (This is the kind of *novelistic* psychological subtlety not easily available to Diderot's dialogue-form.) Julien is an uncannily wise portrait because he is in fact nobler than his egotism. His mantra is 'Each man for himself in this desert of egoism men call life,' a suitably French cynicism. But he can't actually live like this. He is too passionate, too noble. Like Diderot's Rameau, he reveres Tartuffe. But he is nothing like as brilliantly intelligent or all-seeing as the Rameau character, and this is Stendhal's great, novelistic enrichment. Julien poses as a fearsome truth-teller, but he is just an intelligent, under-educated romantic provincial who is not quite clever or supple enough, his mind full of blowsy Napoleonic ardour. We, the readers, can see this. His understanding fluctuates; occasionally he sees clearly, but more often he cannot read upper-class society's codes as well as he thinks he can. He is proudly hypocritical, but not always hypocritical enough to see the need to hide his obvious hypocrisy – he is always blurting out his heart to people when he should keep it closed.

90

In Paris, Julien falls in love with the high-born Mathilde, the daughter of his employer. Each lover wants to be the other's love-slave; but each is also too proud for this, and simultaneously wants to be the other's master. Mathilde is romantically in love with Julien's proud exceptionalism, but feels that it would be beneath her to marry a servant; Julien loves her but is fearful of being patronised. Dostoevsky,

119

writing between the 1840s and 1881, and a keen reader of the French, would become an even greater novelist of the workings of this kind of pride and abasement. There is a direct link from Rousseau to Diderot to Dostoevsky.

In a famous scene in *Notes from Underground*, published in 1864, the narrator, an insignificant but proudly rebellious outcast, has an encounter with an impressive-looking cavalry officer in a tavern. The officer, blocked by the narrator, casually picks him up and moves him out of the way. The narrator is humiliated, and can't sleep for his dreams of revenge. He knows that this same officer walks every day down the Nevsky Prospect. The narrator follows him, 'admiring' him from a distance. He determines that he will walk in the opposite direction and that when the two men meet, he, the narrator, will not budge an inch. But whenever the encounter arrives, he panics, and moves out of the way just as the officer strides past. At night he wakes, obsessively turning over the question: 'Why is it invariably I who swerves first? Why precisely me and not him?' Eventually he holds his ground, the two men brush shoulders, and the narrator is overjoyed. He returns home singing Italian arias, feeling properly avenged. But the satisfaction lasts only a few days.

Dostoevsky was the great analyst – in a sense, almost the inventor – of the psychological category that Nietzsche called *ressentiment*. Again and again, Dostoevsky shows how pride is really very close to humility, and how hate is very close to a kind of sick love, in just the way that Rameau's nephew is far more dependent on the existence of his famous uncle than he will actually admit to, or in the way that Julien both loves and hates Madame de Renal and Mathilde. In the Nevsky Prospect anecdote, the weaker man loathes but 'admires' the officer – and in a sense, loathes him *because* he admires him.

His impotence has less to do with his actual circumstances than with his imaginary relation to the officer, which is one of impotent dependence. Dostoevsky would call this psychological torment the 'Underground', meaning a kind of poisonous, impotent alienation, a chronic instability of self, and a vaunting pride that at any moment might unexpectedly crash into its inverse – cringing self-abasement.[40]

Nothing in fiction, not even in Diderot and Stendhal, quite prepares one for Dostoevsky's characters. In *The Brothers Karamazov*, for instance, the clownish Fyodor Pavlovich is about to enter a dining room at the local monastery. He has already acted terribly in the cell of the saintly monk, Father Zosima. Fyodor decides that he will act scandalously in the dining room also. Why? Because, he thinks to himself, 'it always seems to me, when I go somewhere, that I am lower than everyone else and that they all take me for a buffoon – so let me indeed play the buffoon, because all of you, to a man, are lower than I am.' And as he thinks this, he remembers being asked once why he hated a certain neighbour, to which he had replied: 'He never did anything to me it's true, but I once played a most shame-

---

[40] Dostoevsky's analysis of *ressentiment* has turned out to have great prophetic relevance for the troubles we currently find ourselves in. Terrorism, clearly enough, is the triumph of resentment (sometimes justified); and Dostoevsky's Russian revolutionaries and underground men are essentially terroristic. They dream of hard revenge on a society that seems too soft to deserve sparing. And just as the narrator of *Notes from Underground*, 'admires' the cavalry officer he hates, so perhaps a certain kind of Islamic fundamentalist both hates and 'admires' Western secularism, and hates it because he admires it (hates it, in Dostoevsky's psychological system, *because it once did him a good turn* – gave him medicine, say, or the science that could be used to crash planes into buildings.)

less nasty trick on him, and the moment I did it, I immediately hated him for it.'

91

Dostoevskian character has at least three layers. On the top layer is the announced motive: Raskolnikov, say, proposes several justifications for his murder of the old woman. The second layer involves unconscious motivation, those strange inversions wherein love turns into hate and guilt expresses itself as poisonous, sickly love. Thus Raskolnikov's mad need to confess his crime to the police and to Sonia the prostitute, presages Freud's comment on the action of the superego: 'In many criminals,' writes Freud, 'especially youthful ones, it is possible to detect a very powerful sense of guilt which existed before the crime, and is therefore not its result but its motive.' Or in the case of Fyodor Karamazov and his desire to punish the neighbour whom he was once nasty to, you could say that guilt is causing him, unconsciously, to be horrible to his neighbour; his behaviour recalls the quip – both funny and deadly serious – of the Israeli psychoanalyst who remarked that the Germans would never forgive the Jews for the Holocaust. The third, and bottom layer of motive is beyond explanation and can only be understood religiously. These characters act like this because they want to be *known*; even if they are unaware of it, they want to reveal their baseness; they want to confess. They want to reveal the dark shamefulness of their souls, and so, without knowing quite why, they act 'scandalously' and appallingly in front of others, so that people 'better' than them can judge them for the wretches they are.

There is something deeply philosophical about Dostoevsky's analysis of human behaviour, and Nietzsche and Freud were attracted to his work. (One chapter of Dostoevsky's novella *The Eternal Husband* is entitled 'Analysis'.) Proust, who said that all of Dostoevsky's novels might have the one title, *Crime and Punishment*, studied him with perhaps more care than he would admit to. It is Proust who elaborates and develops the philosophical analysis of psychological motive. In Proust, you can see every element of characterisation – and indeed of fiction-making itself – living happily together, as if you were watching schools of fish underneath a glass-bottomed boat. Thus, his characters are in some sense both externally seen and yet highly inward; they are 'flat', but are extensively analysed by Proust as if they were 'round'; and of course the novel is so massive that their flatness gets elongated over time, and no longer seems like flatness. Proust is not afraid of caricature, and positively loves to 'tag' his characters with leitmotifs, or repeated 'characteristics', in a Dickensian way – as, say, Marcel's grandfather likes repeatedly to say 'On guard! On guard!' and Mme Verdurin always complains of getting a headache whenever music is played. He uses this method to 'fix' his characters, just as the earliest novelists did, or, nearer to his own time, as Dickens, Tolstoy and Mann all did.

But his fiction simultaneously mounts a revolt against the tyranny of fixed, Theophrastan 'characteristics'. Combray is presented as a closed world in which everyone knows everyone else, and Marcel's family is seen as having a supremely secure sense – sustained largely by their system of 'tagging' friends and acquaintances with leitmotifs – of what people are like. When someone informs Marcel's aunt that she has just seen a stranger in the village, she wants to send the maid over to Camus, the chemist,[41] to ask him who this can be: the very notion of someone not known to the family is an outrage. But as Proust puts it, 'our social personality is a creation of the thoughts of other people'. His characters in fact change in unexpected ways, and we must constantly adjust the optic lens which we use to view these people. Marcel's family are sure that they know M. Swann thoroughly; but Proust reveals that they have seen only one side of him, and the least authentic at that. Likewise, Swann falls in love with Odette, because, in part, she reminds him of a woman in a painting; but over the course of many strenuous months, he will find that one of the dangers of love is that it encourages us to fix in our amorous minds a picture of the beloved. Sometimes these alterations are caused by the smallest gestures and revelations, and are in themselves mysterious in origin. Marcel changes his idea of M. Legrandin because he glimpses him talking animatedly to someone and bowing in a peculiar way:

---

[41] Am I the only reader addicted to the utterly foolish pastime of amassing instances in which minor characters in books happen to have the names of writers? Thus Camus the chemist in Proust, and another Camus, this time a grocer, in Bernanos's *Diary of a Country Priest*, and the Pyncheons in *The House of the Seven Gables*, and Horace Updike in *Babbitt*, and Brecht the dentist in *Buddenbrooks*, and Heidegger, one of Trotta's witnesses in Joseph Roth's *The Emperor's Tomb*, and Madame Foucault in Arnold Bennett's *The Old Wives Tale*, and Father Larkin in David Jones's *In Parenthesis*, and Count Tolstoy, a soldier, in *War and Peace*, and a man named Barthès in Rousseau's *Confessions*, and come to think of it, a certain Madame Rousseau in Proust . . .

This rapid straightening-up caused a sort of tense muscular wave to ripple over Legrandin's rump, which I had not supposed to be so fleshy; I cannot say why, but this undulation of pure matter, this wholly carnal fluency devoid of spiritual significance ... awoke my mind suddenly to the possibility of a Legrandin altogether different from the one we knew.[42]

Progress! In Fielding and Defoe, even in the much richer Cervantes, revelation of this altering kind occurs at the level of plot – an unexpected sister, a lost will, and so on. It does not alter our conception of a character. Don Quixote, though an infinitely deep comic *idea*, is the same kind of character at the end of the book as at the beginning. (That is why his deathbed change of heart is so disconcerting.)

93

The Russians and the French essentially set the terms of the modernist novel as it flourished in Britain and America between 1920 and 1945. You can trace the excitement of encounter in Virginia Woolf's essays, especially those written in the teens and the twenties of the century, as she discovers the new translations of the Russians into English by Constance Garnett. She put it like this in 'Mr Bennett and Mrs Brown' (1923):

After reading *Crime and Punishment* and *The Idiot*, how could any young novelist believe in 'characters' as the

---

[42] Proust, *Swann's Way* (Combray).

Victorians had painted them? For the undeniable vividness of so many of them is the result of their crudity. The character is rubbed into us indelibly because its features are so few and so prominent. We are given the keyword [e.g. 'I will never desert Mr Micawber'] and then, since the keyword is astonishingly apt, our imaginations swiftly supply the rest. But what keyword could be applied to Raskolnikov, Mishkin, Stavrogin, or Alyosha? These are characters without any features at all. We go into them as we descend into an enormous cavern.

Ford Madox Ford agreed (though his master was Flaubert). Other than Richardson, he argued in his book *The English Novel*, nothing was worthy of adult attention in English fiction until Henry James came along. For Ford, the serious European novel began with Diderot:

> It was to Diderot – and still more to Stendhal – that the Novel owes its next great step forward ... At that point it became suddenly evident that the Novel as such was capable of being regarded as a means of profoundly serious and many-sided discussion and therefore as a medium of profoundly serious investigation into the human case. It came into its own.

94

This new approach to character meant a new approach to form. When character is stable, form is stable and linear – the novelist begins at the beginning, telling us about his hero's childhood and education, moving decisively forward into the hero's marriage, and then towards the dramatic crux of the book (something is wrong with the marriage). But if character is changeable, then why begin at the beginning? Surely it would be more effective to begin in the middle, and then move backwards, and then move forwards, and then move backwards again? This is just the kind of form Conrad would use in *Lord Jim* and *The Secret Agent*, and Naipaul and Spark in many of their novels.

Is it contradictory to have defended the flatness of characters while simultaneously arguing that the novel has become a more sophisticated analyst of deep, self-divided characters? No, if one resists both Forster's idea of flatness (flatness is more interesting than he makes it out to be) and his idea of roundness (roundness is more complicated than he makes it out to be). In both cases, *subtlety* of analysis is what is important.

SYMPATHY AND COMPLEXITY

95

In 2006, the municipal president of Neza, a tough area of two million people on the eastern edge of Mexico City, decided that the members of his police force needed to become 'better citizens'. He decided that they should be given a reading list, on which could be found *Don Quixote*, Juan Rulfo's beautiful novella *Pedro Páramo*, Octavio Paz's essay on Mexican culture, *The Labyrinth of Solitude*, García Márquez's *One Hundred Years of Solitude*, and works by Carlos Fuentes, Antoine de Saint-Exupéry, Agatha Christie and Edgar Allan Poe.[43]

Neza's chief of police Jorge Amador believes that reading fiction will enrich his officers in at least three ways.

First, by allowing them to acquire a wider vocabulary . . . Next, by granting officers the opportunity to acquire experience by proxy. 'A police officer must be worldly, and books enrich people's experience indirectly.' Finally,

---

[43] See 'Words on the Street' by Angel Gurria-Quintana, in the *Financial Times*, 3 March 2006. I am grateful to Norman Rush for drawing my attention to this article.

Amador claims, there is an ethical benefit. 'Risking your life to save other people's lives and property requires deep convictions. Literature can enhance those deep convictions by allowing readers to discover lives lived with similar commitment. We hope that contact with literature will make our police officers more committed to the values they have pledged to defend.'

How quaintly antique this sounds. Nowadays, the cult of authenticity asserts that nothing is more worldly – more in the world – than police work; thousands of movies and television shows bow to this dogma. The idea the police might get as much or more reality from their armchairs, with their noses in novels, no doubt strikes many as heretically paradoxical.

One does not have to be as morally prescriptive[44] as the Mexican police chief to feel that he has taxonomised three aspects of the experience of reading fiction: language; the world; the extension of our sympathies towards other selves. George Eliot, in her essay on German realism, put it like this: 'The greatest benefit we owe to the artist, whether painter, poet, or novelist, is the extension of our

---

[44] We don't read *in order* to benefit in this way from fiction. We read fiction because it pleases us, moves us, is beautiful, and so on – because it is alive and we are alive. It is amusing to watch evolutionary biology tie itself up in circularities when trying to answer the question 'why do humans spend so much time reading fiction when this yields no obvious evolutionary benefits?' The answers tend either to be utilitarian – we read in order to find out about our fellow citizens, and this has a Darwinian utility – or circular: we read because fiction pushes certain 'pleasure buttons'.

sympathies . . . Art is the nearest thing to life; it is a mode of amplifying experience and extending our contact with our fellowman beyond the bounds of our personal lot.'[45]

Since Plato and Aristotle, fictional and dramatic narrative has provoked two large, recurring discussions: one is centred around the question of mimesis and the real (what should fiction represent?); and the other around the question of sympathy, and how fictional narrative exercises it. Gradually, these two recurrent discussions merge, and one finds that from, say, Samuel Johnson on, it is a commonplace that sympathetic identification with characters is in some way dependent on fiction's true mimesis: to see a world and its fictional people truthfully may expand our capacity for sympathy in the actual world. It is no accident that the novel's rise in the mid-eighteenth century coincides with the rise of the philosophical discussion of sympathy, especially in thinkers like Adam Smith and Shaftesbury. Smith, in *The Theory of Moral Sentiments* (1759), argues what is merely axiomatic today, that 'the source of our fellow-feeling for the misery of others' is mobilised by 'changing places in fancy with the sufferer' – by putting ourselves in others' shoes.

Tolstoy writes about this in *War and Peace*. Before Pierre is taken prisoner by the French, he has had a tendency to see people as hazy groups rather than as particularised individuals, and to feel that he has little free will. After his near-death at their hands (he thinks he is going to be executed), people come alive for him – and he comes alive to himself: 'This legitimate peculiarity of each individual, which used to excite and irritate Pierre, now became a basis of the

---

[45] 'The Natural History of German Life' (1856).

sympathy he felt for, and the interest he took in, other people.'[46]

96

Ian McEwan's *Atonement* is explicitly about the dangers of failing to put oneself in someone else's shoes. The young heroine, Briony, fails in this way in the novel's first section when she wrongly convinces herself that Robbie Turner is a rapist. But putting oneself in another's shoes is what McEwan is signally trying to do as a novelist in this same section, carefully inhabiting one character's point of view after another. Briony's mother, Emily Tallis, stricken with a migraine, lies in bed and thinks anxiously about her children, yet the reader cannot but notice that she is in fact a very bad imaginative sympathiser, because her anxiety and anger get in the way of her sympathy. Reflecting on Cecilia's time at Cambridge, she thinks about her own comparative lack of education, and then quickly, but unwittingly, gets resentful:

> When Cecilia came home in July with her finals' result
> – the nerve of the girl to be disappointed with it! – she
> had no job or skill and still had a husband to find and
> motherhood to confront, and what would her blue-
> stocking teachers – the ones with silly nicknames and
> 'fearsome reputations' – have to tell her about that?
> Those self-important women gained local immortality
> for the blandest, the most timid of eccentricities –

---

[46] Tolstoy, *War and Peace*, Book Four, Part Four, chapter 13.

walking a cat on a dog's lead, riding about on a man's bike, being seen with a sandwich in the street. A generation later these silly, ignorant ladies would be long dead and still revered at High Table and spoken of in lowered voices.

In Adam Smith's terms, Emily is quite unable to 'change places' with her daughter; in a novelist's or actor's language, she is no good at 'being' Cecilia. But of course McEwan is himself wonderfully good here at 'being' Emily Tallis, using free indirect style with perfect poise to inhabit her complicated envy.

Later in the section, as Emily sits by the light, she sees moths drawn to it, and recalls being told by 'a professor of some science or another' that

> it was the visual impression of an even deeper darkness beyond the light that drew them in. Even though they might be eaten, they had to obey the instinct that made them seek out the darkest place, on the far side of the light – and in this case it was an illusion. It sounded to her like sophistry, or an explanation for its own sake. How could anyone presume to know the world through the eyes of an insect?

Emily *would* think this.

McEwan knowingly alludes to a celebrated dilemma in the philosophy of consciousness, most famously raised by Thomas Nagel in his essay 'What is it like to be a bat?' Nagel concludes that a human cannot change places with a bat, that imaginative transfer on the part of a human is impossible: 'Insofar as I can imagine this (which is not very far), it tells me only what it would be like for me to behave as a bat behaves. But that is not the question. I want to know what it is like for a bat to be a bat.'[47] Standing up for novelists, as it were, J. M. Coetzee has his novelist-heroine, Elizabeth Costello, explicitly reply to Nagel in his eponymous novel. Costello says that imagining what it is like to be a bat would simply be the definition of a good novelist. I can imagine being a corpse, says Costello, why can I not then imagine being a bat? (Tolstoy, again, in an electrifying moment at the end of his novella *Hadji Murad*, imagines what it might be like to have one's head cut off, and for consciousness to persist for a second or two in the brain even as the head has left the body. His imaginative insight foreshadows modern neuroscience, which does indeed suggest that consciousness can continue for a minute or two in a severed head.)

97

The philosopher Bernard Williams was exercised by the inadequacy of moral philosophy.[48] He found that much of it, descending from Kant, essentially wrote the messiness of the self out of philosophical discussion. Philosophy, he thought, tended to view conflicts as conflicts of beliefs that could be easily solved, rather than as conflicts of desires that are not so easily solved. One example he used, in his book *Moral Luck*, was that of a man who has promised his father, after

---

[47] 'What Is it Like to Be a Bat?' in *Mortal Questions* (1974).
[48] See, especially, *Problems of the Self* (1973), *Moral Luck* (1981), and *Making Sense of Humanity* (1995).

his father's death, that he will support a favoured charity with his inheritance. But the son finds that, as time goes on, there is not enough money for him to fulfill his promise to his father and also look after his own children. A certain kind of moral philosopher, wrote Williams, would decide that one way to resolve this conflict is to say that the son had good reason to assume, as a tacit condition of the inheritance, that he should only give money to the charity after more immediate pressing concerns, like his children, were taken care of. The conflict is resolved by nullifying one of its elements.

Williams thought that Kantians had a tendency to treat all conflicts of obligation like this, whereas Williams was interested in what he called 'tragic dilemmas', in which someone is faced with two conflicting moral requirements, each equally pressing. Agamemnon either betrays his army or sacrifices his daughter; either action will cause him lasting regret and shame. For Williams, moral philosophy needed to attend to the actual fabric of emotional life, instead of talking about the self, in Kantian terms, as consistent, principled and universal. No, said Williams, people are inconsistent; they make up their principles as they go along; and they are determined by all kinds of things – genetics, upbringing, society, and so on.

Williams often returned to Greek tragedy and epic for examples of great stories in which we see the self struggling with what he called 'one-person conflicts'. Curiously, he rarely if ever talked about the novel, perhaps because the novel tends to present such tragic conflicts less starkly, less tragically, in softened forms. Yet these softer conflicts are not the less interesting or profound for being softer: consider – just to pluck one kind of struggle – what extraordinary empirical insight the novel has given us into marriage and all its conflicts, both two-person (between spouses) and one-person (the lonely individual suffering inside a loveless or mistaken union). Consider *To the Lighthouse*, so moving in part because it is an account not of a brilliantly successful marriage nor of an incandescently failed one, but of an adequate one, in which struggles and little compromises are daily enacted. Here, Mr and Mrs Ramsay walk in the garden and talk about their son:

> They paused. He wished Andrew could be induced to work harder. He would lose every chance of a scholar-ship if he didn't. 'Oh, scholarships!' she said. Mr Ramsay thought her foolish for saying that about a serious thing like a scholarship. He should be very proud of Andrew if he got a scholarship, he said. She would be just as proud of him if he didn't, she answered. They disagreed always about this, but it did not matter. She liked him to believe in scholarships, and he liked her to be proud of Andrew whatever he did.

The subtlety lies in the picture of each side disagreeing, but wanting nonetheless the other to remain the same.

Of course, the novel does not provide philosophical answers (as Chekhov said, it only needs to ask the right ques-tions). Instead, it does what Williams wanted moral phil-osophy to do – it gives the best account of the complexity of our moral fabric. When Pierre, in *War and Peace*, begins to change his ideas about himself and other people, he realises that the only way to understand people properly is to see things from each person's point of view: 'There was a new feature in Pierre's relations with Willarski, with the princess, with the doctor, and with all the people he now met, which gained for him the general goodwill. This was his acknowledgement of the impossibility of changing a man's convictions by words, and his recognition of the possibility of everyone thinking, feeling, and seeing things each from his own point of view . . . The difference, and sometimes complete contradiction, between men's opinions and their lives, and between one man and another, pleased him and evoked from him an amused and gentle smile.'[49]

---

[49] Tolstoy, *War and Peace*, Book Four, Part Four, Chapter 13.

LANGUAGE

98

The poet Glyn Maxwell likes to conduct the following test in his writing classes, one apparently used by Auden. He gives them Philip Larkin's poem 'The Whitsun Weddings', with certain words blacked out. He tells them what kinds of words – nouns, verbs, adjectives – have been omitted, and how they complete the metre of the line. The aspiring poets must try to fill the blanks. Larkin is travelling by train from the north of England to London, and as he watches from the window, he records passing sights. One of these is a hothouse, which he renders: 'A hothouse flashed uniquely.' Maxwell excises 'uniquely', telling his students that a tri-syllabic adverb is missing. Not once has a student supplied 'uniquely'. 'Uniquely' is unique.

99

Nietzsche laments, in *Beyond Good and Evil*: 'What a torment books written in German are for him who has a *third ear*.' If prose is to be as well written as poetry – the old modernist hope – novelists and readers must develop their own third ears. We have to read musically, testing the precision and rhythm of a sentence, listening for the almost inaudible rustle of historical association clinging to the hems of modern words, attending to patterns, repetitions, echoes, deciding why a metaphor is successful and another is not, judging how the perfect placement of the right verb or adjective seals a sentence with mathematical finality. We must proceed on the assumption that almost all prose popularly acclaimed as beautiful ('she writes like an angel') is nothing of the sort, that almost every novelist will at some point be baselessly acclaimed for writing 'beautifully' as almost all flowers are at some point acclaimed for smelling nice.

100

There is a way in which even complex prose is quite simple – because of that mathematical finality by which a perfect sentence cannot admit of an infinite number of variations, cannot be extended without aesthetic blight: its perfection is the solution to its own puzzle; it could not be done better.

There is a familiar American simplicity, for instance, which is Puritan and colloquial in origin, 'a sort of ecstatic fire that takes things down to the essentials', as Marilynne Robinson has it in her novel *Gilead*. We recognise it in the Puritan sermon, in Jonathan Edwards, in Ulysses S. Grant's memoirs, in Mark Twain, in Willa Cather, in Hemingway. These are the obvious examples. But that same simplicity is also always present in much more ornate writers like Melville, Emerson, Cormac McCarthy. 'The stars fall all night in bitter arcs.' 'The horses stepped archly among the shadows that fell over the road.' These lucid phrases are from McCarthy's *Blood*

Meridian and *All the Pretty Horses*, respectively, books whose prose is often fantastically baroque. Marilynne Robinson's novel *Gilead* achieves an almost holy simplicity; but this is the same writer whose earlier novel, *Housekeeping*, abounds in complicated Melvillean metaphor and analogy. Is the following passage from *Gilead* an example of simple or complicated prose?

> This morning a splendid dawn passed over our house on its way to Kansas. This morning Kansas rolled out of its sleep into a sunlight grandly announced, proclaimed throughout heaven – one more of the very finite number of days that this old prairie has been called Kansas, or Iowa. But it has all been one day, that first day. Light is constant, we just turn over in it. So every day is in fact the selfsame evening and morning. My grandfather's grave turned into the light, and the dew on his weedy little mortality patch was glorious.

Weedy little mortality patch – how fine that is.

101

Prose is always simple *in this sense*, because language is the ordinary medium of daily communication – unlike music or paint. Our ordinary possessions are being borrowed by even very difficult writers: the millionaires of style – difficult, lavish stylists like Sir Thomas Browne, Melville, Ruskin, Lawrence, James, Woolf – are very prosperous, but they use the same banknotes as everyone else. 'Vague squares of rich colour' is the simple little formulation Henry James uses to describe Old Master paintings seen from a distance in a darkened room in *The Portrait of a Lady*. How precise, paradoxically, is that 'vague'! Aren't these exactly the best words in the best order? 'The day waves yellow with all its crops.' That is Woolf, from *The Waves*. I am consumed by this sentence, partly because I cannot quite explain why it moves me so much. I can see, hear, its beauty, its strangeness. Its music is very simple. Its words are simple. And its *meaning* is simple, too. Woolf is describing the sun rising and finally filling the day with its yellow fire. The sentence means something like: this is what a field of corn on a summer's day will look like when everything is blazing with sunlight – a yellow semaphore, a sea of moving colour. We *know* exactly and instantly what Woolf means, and we think: that could not be put any better. The secret lies in the decision to avoid the usual image of crops waving, and instead, to write *the day waves*: the effect is suddenly that the day itself, the very fabric and temporality of the day, seems saturated in yellow. And then that peculiar, apparently nonsensical *waves yellow* (how can anything wave yellow?) conveys a sense that yellowness has so intensely taken over the day itself that it has taken over our verbs, too – yellowness has conquered our agency. How do we wave? We wave yellow. That is all we can do. The sunlight is so absolute that it stuns us, makes us sluggish, robs us of will. Eight simple words evoke colour, high summer, warm lethargy, ripeness.

102

In *Sea and Sardinia*, Lawrence describes the short legs of King Victor Emmanuel; but he refers to 'his little short legs'. Now, in some technical sense, there is no need to have both 'short' and 'little' in the same sentence. If Lawrence were a schoolboy, his teacher would write 'redundant' in the margin and remove one of the adjectives. But say it aloud a few times, and it suddenly seems inevitable. We need the two words, because they sound farcical together. And short does not mean the same as little: the two words enjoy each other's company; and 'little short legs' is more original than 'short little legs' because it is jumpier, is more absurd, forcing us to stumble slightly – stumble short-leggedly – over the unexpected rhythm.

103

We cannot write about rhythm and not refer to Flaubert, and so once again, as if unable to stop rereading the old letters of a former lover, I return to him. Of course writers before him had agonised about style. But no novelist agonised as much or as publicly, no novelist fetishised the poetry of 'the sentence' in the same way, no novelist pushed to such an extreme the potential alienation of form and content (Flaubert longed to write what he called a 'book about nothing'). And no novelist before Flaubert reflected as self-consciously on questions of technique. With Flaubert, literature became 'essentially problematic', as one scholar puts it.[50]

---

[50] Stephen Heath, in *Madame Bovary* (1998).

Or just modern? Flaubert himself affected a nostalgia for the great unselfconscious writers who came before him, the beasts of instinct who just got on with it, like Molière and Cervantes; they, said Flaubert in his letters, 'had no techniques'. He, on the other hand, was betrothed to 'atrocious labour' and 'fanaticism'. This fanaticism was applied to the music and rhythm of the sentence. In different ways, the modern novelist is shadowed by that monkish labour. The rich stylist – the Bellow, the Updike – is made newly self-conscious about his richness; but the plainer stylist – Hemingway, for example – has also become self-conscious about his plainness, itself now resembling a form of highly controlled and minimalist richness, a stylishness of renunciation. The realist feels Flaubert breathing down his neck: is it well written enough? But the formalist or postmodernist is also indebted to Flaubert for the dream of a book about nothing, a book flying high on style alone. (Alain Robbe-Grillet and Nathalie Sarraute, originators of the *nouveau roman*, were explicit about crediting Flaubert as their great precursor.)

Flaubert loved to read aloud. It took him thirty-two hours to read his overblown lyrical fantasia *The Temptation of Saint Anthony* to two friends. And when he dined in Paris at the Goncourts, he loved to read out examples of bad writing. Turgenev said that he knew of 'no other writer who scrupled in quite that way'. Even Henry James, the master stylist, was somewhat appalled by the religious devotion with which Flaubert assassinated repetition, unwanted clichés, clumsy sonorities. The scene of his writing has become notorious: the study at Croisset, the slow river outside the window while inside the bearish Norman, wrapped in his dressing gown and wreathed in pipe smoke, groaned and complained about

142

how slow his progress was, each sentence laid as slowly and agonisingly as a fuse.[51]

So what did Flaubert mean by style, by the music of a sentence? This, from *Madame Bovary* – Charles is stupidly proud that he has got Emma pregnant: 'L'idée d'avoir engendré le délectait.' So compact, so precise, so rhythmic. Literally, this is 'The idea of having engendered delighted him.' Geoffrey Wall, in his Penguin translation, renders it as: 'The thought of having impregnated her was delectable to him.' This is good, but pity the poor translator. For the English is a wan cousin of the French. Say the French out aloud, as Flaubert would have done, and you encounter four 'ay' sounds in three of the words: 'l'id*ée*, engend*ré*, d*él*ect*ait*.' An English translation that tried to mimic the untranslatable music of the French – that tried to mimic the rhyming – would sound like bad hip-hop: 'The not*ion* of procrea*tion* was a delecta*tion*.'

104

Yet even if Flaubertianism casts a permanent shadow over the development of style in fiction, our sense of what is

---

[51] Though one wonders if a great deal of time was not spent just sleeping and masturbating (Flaubert likened sentences to ejaculate). Often, the excruciation of the stylist seems to be a front for writer's block. This was the case with the marvellous American writer J. F. Powers, for instance, of whom Sean O'Faolain joked, in Wildean fashion, that he 'spent the morning putting in a comma and the afternoon wondering whether or not he should replace it with a semicolon'. More usual, I think, is the kind of literary routine ascribed to the minor English writer A. C. Benson – that he did nothing all morning and then spent the afternoon writing up what he'd done in the morning.

musical in style constantly changes. Flaubert feared repetition, but of course Hemingway and Lawrence would make repetition the basis of their most beautiful effects. Here is Lawrence, again, in *Sea and Sardinia*:

> Very dark under the great carob tree as we go down the steps. Dark still the garden. Scent of mimosa, and then of jasmine. The lovely mimosa tree invisible. Dark the stony path. The goat whinnies out of her shed. The broken Roman tomb which lolls right over the garden track does not fall on me as I slip under its massive tilt. Ah, dark garden, dark garden, with your olives and your wine, your medlars and mulberries and many almond trees, your steep terraces ledged high up above the sea, I am leaving you, slinking out. Out between the rosemary hedges, out of the tall gate, on to the cruel steep stony road. So under the dark, big eucalyptus trees, over the stream, and up towards the village. There, I have got so far.

Lawrence is leaving a Sicilian house at dawn, and heading for the ferry: 'I am leaving you, slinking out.' This is his farewell to all that he has loved there. The passage might as well be an example of simplicity as of musicality. Its complexity, such as it is, lies in his attempt to use his prose to register, minute by minute, the painful largo of this farewell. Each sentence slows down to make its own farewell: 'Scent of mimosa, and then of jasmine. The lovely mimosa tree invisible.' First you smell the scent, then you see – or apprehend – the tree. After that, the path. Sentence by sentence.

And meanwhile the darkness is changing as the day breaks, which is why Lawrence repeats his word 'dark.' In fact, every time he repeats the word, the word has changed a little, because each time Lawrence changes what he attaches the word 'dark' to: *very dark, dark still, dark the, dark garden, the dark, big eucalyptus trees*. Repetition is not really repetition after all. It is alteration: dawn light is slowly dissolving this darkness. At the end of it all, the writer has done no more than get onto the path: 'There, I have got so far.' This could be a description of the movement of the prose, too. So near, so far. So little, so much.

105

Listen to the operation of an intensely musical ear in one of the greatest stylists of American prose, Saul Bellow, a writer who makes even the fleet-footed – the Updikes, the DeLillos, the Roths – seem like monopodes. Like all serious novelists, Bellow read poetry: Shakespeare first (he could recite lines and lines from the plays, remembered from his schooldays in Chicago), then Milton, Keats, Wordsworth, Hardy, Larkin, and his friend John Berryman. And behind all this, with its English stretching all the way back into deeper antiquity, the King James Bible. A river, seen as 'crimped, green, blackish, glassy', or Chicago as 'blue with winter, brown with evening, crystal with frost', or New York as 'sheer walls, gray spaces, dry lagoons of tar and pebbles'. Here is a paragraph from his story 'The Old System', in which Isaac Braun, in a high state of agitation, rushes to get his plane at Newark airport.

On the airport bus, he opened his father's copy of the Psalms. The black Hebrew letters only gaped at him like open mouths with tongues hanging down, pointing upward, flaming but dumb. He tried – forcing. It did no good. The tunnel, the swamps, the auto skeletons, machine entrails, dumps, gulls, sketchy Newark trembling in fiery summer, held his attention minutely . . . Then in the jet running with concentrated fury to take off – the power to pull away from the magnetic earth; and more: When he saw the ground tilt backward, the machine rising from the runway, he said to himself in clear internal words, '*Shema Yisrael*,' Hear, O Israel, God alone is God! On the right, New York leaned gigantically seaward, and the plane with a jolt of retracted wheels turned toward the river. The Hudson green within green, and rough with tide and wind. Isaac released the breath he had been holding, but sat belted tight. Above the marvelous bridges, over clouds, sailing in atmosphere, you know better than ever that you are no angel.

Bellow had a habit of writing repeatedly about flying, partly, I guess, because it was the great obvious advantage he had over his dead competitors, those writers who had never seen the world from above the clouds: Melville, Tolstoy, Proust. And how well he does it! Notice, first of all, that the rhythm of the passage never settles down. Bellow gets a list going, with a repeated 'the', and then suddenly drops 'the' halfway through: '*The* tunnels, *the* swamps, *the* auto skeletons,/ machine entrails, dumps, gulls, sketchy Newark . . .' The effect is destabilising, agitating. (Thus even this passage is a version of free indirect style, striving to capture or mimic Isaac Braun's flustered anxiety, his eye failing to retain things seen through the bus window.) And in sentence after sentence the world is captured with brimming novelty: Newark seen as 'sketchy' and 'trembling in fiery summer', the jet 'running with concentrated fury to take off' (a phrase that with its unpunctuated onrush itself enacts such a concentrated fury), New York which, as the plane tilts, 'leaned gigantically seaward' (say the phrase aloud, and see how the words themselves – 'leaned gi-gan-tic-ally sea-ward' – elongate the experience, so that the very language embodies the queasiness it describes); the dainty, unexpected rhythm of 'The Hudson green within green, and rough with tide and wind' ('green within green' captures very precisely the different shades of green that we see in large bodies of cold water when several thousand feet above them); and finally, 'sailing in atmosphere' – isn't that exactly what the freedom of flight feels like? And yet until this moment one did not have these words to fit this feeling. Until this moment, one was comparatively inarticulate; until this moment, one had been blandly inhabiting a deprived eloquence.

How does this kind of stylishness avoid the dilemma we explored earlier, in Flaubert and Updike and David Foster Wallace, in which the stylish novelist uses words that his more hapless fictional character could never have come up with? It doesn't. The tension is still there, and Bellow has to remind us that Newark 'held his [Isaac's] attention minutely', as if to say, 'You see, Isaac really is looking as hard as I am at these things.' But Bellow's details and rhythms are so mobile, so dynamic, that they seem less vulnerable to the charge of aestheticism than do Flaubert's or Updike's. That smooth, pre-made wall of prose that Flaubert wanted us to gasp at – 'How does it all come about?' – is here a rougher lattice, through which we seem to see a style apparently in the process of being made. This roughened-up texture and rhythm is, for me at least, one of the reasons that I rarely find Bellow an intrusive lyricist, despite his high stylishness.[52]

106

One way to tell slick genre prose from really interesting writing is to look, in the former case, for the absence of different registers. An efficient thriller will often be written in a style that is locked into place: the musical analogue of this might be a tune, proceeding in unison, the melody separated only by octave intervals, without any harmony in the middle. By contrast, rich and daring prose avails itself of harmony and dissonance by being able to move in and out of place. In writing, a 'register' is nothing more than a name for a kind of diction, which is nothing more than a name for a certain, distinctive way of saying something – so we talk about 'high' and 'low' registers (e.g. the high-ish 'Father' and the lower 'Pop'), grand and vernacular diction, mock-heroic diction, clichéd registers, and so on.

We have a conventional expectation that prose should be written in only one, unvarying register – a solid block, like everyone agreeing to wear black at a funeral. But this is a social convention, and eighteenth-century prose, for instance, is especially good at subverting this expectation, wringing comedy out of the jostling together of different

[52] Lukács, in *Studies in European Realism*, distinguishes between the frozen detail of Flaubert and Zola, and the more dynamic detail of Tolstoy, Shakespeare and Balzac. Lukács borrowed this idea from Lessing's *Laocoön*, in which Lessing praises Homer's description of Achilles' shield, not as something finished and complete, but 'as a shield that is being made'.

registers that we had not thought should share the same family space. We saw how well Jane Austen made fun of Sir William Lucas, by writing that he built a new house, 'denominated from that period Lucas Lodge'. With the phrase 'denominated from that period', and especially the fancy verb 'denominated', Austen uses a grand register (or pompous diction) to mock Sir William's own pomposity. More subtly, in *Emma*, Mrs Elton, on the trip to Donwell Abbey to pick strawberries, is described as dressed in 'all her apparatus of happiness, her large bonnet and her basket'. The phrase 'apparatus of happiness' is of course absolutely killing, and, as in the Lucas Lodge passage, the comedy emanates from the little lift in register, the move upwards, to that word 'apparatus'. Suggestive of technical efficiency, the word belongs to a scientific register that puts it at odds with 'of happiness'. An apparatus of happiness sounds more like an inverted torture machine than a bonnet and basket, and it promises a kind of doggedness, a persistence, that fits Mrs Elton's character, and which makes the heart sink.

Austen's tricks can be found in modern writers as different as Muriel Spark and Philip Roth. In *The Prime of Miss Jean Brodie*, one of the little girls, Jenny, is confronted one day by a flasher; or as Spark wittily has it, 'was accosted by a man joyfully exposing himself beside the Water of Leith'. That adverb, 'joyfully', is marvellously unexpected, and seems to have no place in the sentence. It robs the incident of menace, and makes it almost a fairy tale. The capitalised 'Water of Leith' introduces an absurd mock-heroic register that Pope would have applauded. The Water of Leith is a small river; to insist on identifying it makes further fun of the incident, and the aural suggestion of Lethe is very funny.

149

You can hear the comedy in these different dictions – and laugh – without necessarily knowing why.[53]

Philip Roth does something similar in this long sentence from *Sabbath's Theater*. Mickey Sabbath, satanic seducer and misanthrope, has been having a long, juicy affair with a Croatian-American, Drenka:

> Lately, when Sabbath suckled at Drenka's uberous breasts – uberous, the root word of *exuberant*, which is itself *ex* plus *uberare*, to be fruitful, to overflow like Juno lying prone in Tintoretto's painting where the Milky Way is coming out of her tit – suckled with an unrelenting frenzy that caused Drenka to roll her head ecstatically back and to groan (as Juno herself may have once groaned), 'I feel it deep down in my cunt,' he was pierced by the sharpest of longings for his late little mother.

What an amazingly blasphemous little mélange that is. This sentence is really dirty, and partly because it conforms to

<hr>

[53] It is partly by shifts in register that we gain a sense of a human *voice* speaking to us – Austen's, Spark's, Roth's. Likewise, by dancing between registers a character sounds real to us, whether Hamlet or Leopold Bloom. Movements in diction capture some of the waywardness and roominess of actual thinking: David Foster Wallace and Norman Rush exploit this to considerable effect. Rush's two novels, *Mating* and *Mortals*, are full of the most fantastic shifts in diction, and the effect is the creation of a real, but strange, American voice, at once overeducated and colloquial: 'This jeu maintained its facetious character, but there came a time when I began to resent it as a concealed way of short-circuiting my episode of depression, because he preferred me to be merry, naturally.' Or: 'I was manic and global. Everything was a last straw. I went up the hill on passivity and down again.'

the well-known definition of dirt – matter out of place, which is itself a definition of the mixing of high and low dictions. But why would Roth engage in such baroque deferrals and shifts? Why write it so complicatedly? If you render the simple matter of his sentence and keep everything in place – i.e., remove the jostle of registers – you see why. A simple version would go like this: 'Lately, when Sabbath sucked Drenka's breasts, he was pierced by the sharpest of longings for his late mother.' It is still funny, because of the slide from lover to mother, but it is not *exuberant*. So the first thing the complexity achieves is to enact the exuberance, the hasty joy and chaotic desire, of sex. Secondly, the long, mock-pedantic, suspended subclause about the Latin origin of uberous and Tintoretto's painting of Juno, works, in proper music-hall fashion, to delay the punchline of 'he was pierced by the sharpest of longings for his late little *mother*.' (It also delays, and makes more shocking and unexpected, the entrance of 'cunt'.) Third, since the comedy of the subject-matter of the sentence involves moving from one register to another – from a lover's breast to a mother's – it is fitting that the style of the sentence mimics this scandalous shift, by engaging in its own stylistic shifts, going up and down like a manic ECG: so we have 'suckled' (high diction), 'breasts' (medium), *uberare* (high), Tintoretto's painting (high), 'where the Milky Way is coming out of her tit' (low), 'unrelenting frenzy' (high, rather formal diction), 'as Juno herself may have once groaned' (still quite high), 'cunt' (very low), 'pierced by the sharpest of longings' (high, formal diction again). By insisting on equalising all these different levels of diction, the style of the sentence works as style should, to incarnate the meaning, and the meaning itself, of course, is all about the scandal of equalising different registers. *Sabbath's Theater* is a passionate, intensely funny, repellent and very moving portrait of the scandal of male sexuality, which is repeatedly linked in the book to vitality itself. To be able to have an erection in the morning, to be able to seduce women in one's mid-sixties, to be able to persist in scandalising bourgeois morality, to be able to say every single day, as the ageing Mickey does, 'Fuck the laudable ideologies!' is to be alive. And this sentence is utterly alive, and is alive by virtue of the way it scandalises proper norms. Is it Drenka or Juno or Mickey's late mother who is being fucked in this sentence? All three of them. Roth brilliantly catches the needy, babyish side of male sexuality, in which a lover's breast is still really mommy's suckling tit, because mommy was your first and only lover. Drenka, then, inevitably, is both Madonna (mother, Juno) and whore (because she can't be as good as mommy was). In classic misogynistic fashion, the woman is adored and hated by men because she is the source of life – the Milky Way flows out of her breasts, and children come from between her legs ('the Monster of the Beginning Womb', as Allen Ginsberg calls it in *Kaddish*). Men cannot rival that, even as they, like Mickey or late Yeats, rage on about male 'vitality'. And notice the subtle way that, with his verb 'pierced' ('pierced by the sharpest of longings'), Roth inverts the presumed male–female order. Mickey, who is presumably *piercing* (in a sexual sense) this mother-whore by *entering* her, is really being *pierced* or entered – fucked back in turn – by the woman who gave birth to him. All this in one superb sentence.

Metaphor is analogous to fiction, because it floats a rival reality. It is the entire imaginative process in one move. If I compare the slates on a roof to an armadillo's back, or – as I did earlier – the bald patch on the top of my head to a crop circle (or on very bad days, to the kind of flattened ring of grass that a helicopter's blades make when it lands in a field), I am asking you to do what Conrad said fiction should make you do – *see*. I am asking you to imagine another dimension, to picture a likeness. Every metaphor or simile is a little explosion of fiction within the larger fiction of the novel or story. Near the end of *The Rainbow*, Ursula looks out at London from her hotel balcony. It is dawn, and 'the lamps of Piccadilly, stringing away beside the trees of the park, were becoming pale and moth-like'. Pale and moth-like! We know, in a flash, exactly what Lawrence means, but we had not *seen* those lights like moths until this moment.

And of course this explosion of fiction-within-fiction is not exclusively visual, any more than detail in fiction is exclusively visual. 'As he spoke he stroked both sides of his mutton-chop whiskers as if he wished to caress simultaneously both halves of the monarchy.' That is from Joseph Roth's novel *The Radetzky March*, which chronicles the decline of a family in the last years of the Austro-Hungarian empire. The two halves of the monarchy, then, are the Austrian side and the Hungarian side. It is a fantastical image, excitingly surreal and strange, but you could not say that the simile brings the two halves of the whiskers to our eye, any more than Shakespeare (or his co-writer) intends us to visualise something when a fisherman in *Pericles* exclaims: 'here's a fish hangs in the net like a poor man's right in the law'. Instead, Roth's is the kind of hypothetical or analogical – 'as if' – metaphor that Shakespeare is very fond of. It wittily tells us something about the devotion of this Hapsburg bureaucrat; it arrests him in an outlandishly symbolic gesture.

108

Wittgenstein once complained that Shakespeare's similes were *'in the ordinary sense*, bad'.[54] Doubtless he meant Shakespeare's fondness for metaphorical extravagance, and his tendency to mix his metaphors, as when Henry complains about 'the moody frontier of a servant brow' in *Henry IV, Part 1*. There are readers who will object that a brow cannot be a frontier, and that a frontier cannot be moody. But again, as in the Lawrence example, metaphor is doing here what it is supposed to do; it is speeding us, imaginatively, towards a new meaning. A better example – also involving a brow – occurs in *Macbeth*, when Macbeth is watching his wife sleepwalking, and implores the doctor to help her: 'Raze out [i.e. erase] the written troubles of the brain.' Wittgenstein would not approve, but Wittgenstein was not, in the end, a very literary reader. That strange image manages to combine the idea of our trouble as a sentence of judgement, 'written' by the Gods; the customary idea of the mind as a book upon which are written our thoughts; and the idea of the lines on a troubled brow, lines written

---

[54] *Culture and Value*, ed. G. H. Von Wright and Heikki Nyman, trans. Peter Winch (1980).

into the brow by distress. Readers and theatre-goers storm upon these meanings in a flash, without having to unpack them in the laborious way I have just done.

Actually, there is a way in which mixed metaphor is perfectly logical, and not an aberration at all. After all, metaphor is already a mixing of disparate agents – a brow is not really like a frontier – and so mixed metaphor can be said to be the essence, the hypostasis, of metaphor: if a brow can be like a frontier, it follows that a frontier can be moody. In contemporary parlance, what people dislike about mixed metaphor is that it tends to combine two different *clichés*, as in, say, 'out of a sea of despair, he has pulled forth a plum'. The metaphorical aspect is actually dimmed, almost to non-existence, by the presence of two or more mixed clichés (which by definition are themselves dim or dead metaphors). But Shakespeare's metaphors more often inhabit a speculative realm rather than a mechanical one, in which readers and audience have already been asked to abandon a customary world of familiar correspondence (as, for instance, when Macbeth likens pity to a new-born babe). Henry James was once reproved for using mixed metaphors in a novel, and he replied to his correspondent that he used not mixed but 'loose metaphors': 'Lastly, the metaphor about muffling shame in a splendor that asks no questions is indeed a trifle mixed; but it is essentially a loose metaphor – it isn't a simile – it doesn't pretend to sail close to the wind.'[55] (And notice that the inveterately metaphorical James has to provide

---

[55] Letter to Grace Norton, March 1876, in *Henry James: A Life in Letters*, edited by Philip Horne (1999).

155

another metaphor, about sailing close to the wind, to explain his own metaphors.)[56]

But most simile and metaphor, certainly of the visual kind, does pretend, of course, to sail close to the wind, and gives us that sense that something has been newly painted before our eyes. Here, for instance, are four metaphorical descriptions of fire, all of them tremendously successful. Lawrence, seeing a fire in a grate, writes of it as 'that rushing bouquet of new flames in the grate' (*Sea and Sardinia*). Hardy describes 'a scarlet handful of fire' in Gabriel Oak's cottage in *Far from the Madding Crowd*. Bellow has this sentence about a fire in his story 'A Silver Dish': 'The blue flames fluttered like a school of fishes in the coal fire.' And Norman Rush, in his novel *Mortals*, which is set in Botswana, has his hero come upon an abandoned village, where he sees that 'cooking fires wagged in some of the lalwapas' (a lalwapa is a kind of simple African courtyard). So: a rushing bouquet (DHL); a handful of scarlet fire (TH); a school of fishes (SB), and a wagging fire (NR). Is one better than the others? Each works slightly differently. The Bellow and the Lawrence are perhaps the most visual – we can see in our mind's eye the flames as bright as flowers and rippling like fish (notice that Bellow writes 'a school of fishes' not 'a school of fish', precisely because the plural sounds more numerous, more rippling). Hardy is the most homely, perhaps, but very daring

---

[56] James can, when he wants to, sail close to the wind in simile, thus nicely disproving Nabokov's slanderous complaint to Edmund Wilson. In *The American Scene*, written in 1907, he likens the already crowded Manhattan skyline to a pincushion whose pins have been put in at night-time, any old how. Later in the same book he compares it to an upturned comb, with teeth missing.

in his way: we might think of a handful of dust but never of a handful of fire, since we keep our hands away from fire. Rush's is marvellous. Flame does indeed wag (i.e. bend, flap, dip, decrease, increase), but when would most of us ever think to use the verb 'wag'? Like Hardy's handful, wag is daring precisely because it is a strikingly unfiery verb. Tails wag, and jokers are called wags, but flame belongs to a different realm from this cosiness. Lawrence's is the most verbally daring, because, along with the likening of flames to a bouquet of flowers (and of course, flames are indeed gathered in a grate for us as a bouquet gathers flowers in a vase), there is the pairing of 'rushing' with 'bouquet' – 'a rushing bouquet' – which is a further metaphor within the larger metaphor, since while flames can rush at us, bouquets cannot. In a way, it is a mixed metaphor. So Lawrence is the only writer in this group to give us two metaphors for the price of one. (*New* flames, to go with the idea of new flowers, perhaps introduces a third.)

These four examples tell us that often the leap towards the counter-intuitive, towards the very opposite of the thing you are seeking to compare, is the secret of powerful metaphor. Flame is as far from flowers, fish, handfuls and wagging as can be imagined. Clearly this is the principle, if not quite the effect, of the technique made famous by the Russian formalists, *ostranenie*, or defamiliarisation. Céline, in his novel *Journey to the End of the Night*, shocks us out of the familiar by likening rush hour in Paris to catastrophe: 'Seeing them all fleeing in that direction you'd think that there must have been some catastrophe at Argenteuil, that the town was on fire.' Nabokov, showing his Symbolist and formalist roots, likens a rainbow-coloured oil-slick in *The Gift* to 'Asphalt's parakeet'. Obviously, whenever you extravagantly liken x to y, and a large gap exists between x and y, you will be drawing attention to the fact that x is really nothing like y, as well as drawing attention to the effort involved in producing such extravagances.

The kind of metaphor I most delight in, however, like the ones above about fire, estranges and then instantly connects, and in doing the latter so well, hides the former. The result is a tiny shock of surprise, followed by a feeling of inevitability. In *To the Lighthouse*, Mrs Ramsay says good-night to her children, and carefully closes the bedroom door, and lets 'the tongue of the door slowly lengthen in the lock'. The metaphor in that sentence lies not so much in 'tongue', which is fairly conventional (since people do talk about locks having tongues) but is secretly buried in the verb, 'length-ened'. That verb *lengthens* the whole procedure: isn't this the best description you have ever read of someone very sl-o-w-ly turning a handle of a door so as not to waken children? (Tongue is good, too, because tongues make noise, while this particular tongue has to stay silent. And the now bliss-fully silent children have of course been using their noisy tongues all day.) In the opposite spirit, in Katherine Mansfield's 'Daughters of the Late Colonel', Kate, the cook, has a habit of 'bursting through the door in her usual fashion, as though she had discovered some secret panel'. It would take the repetition of weekly episodes, and the full panoply of actors and set, to reproduce, in Kramer's similar antics on *Seinfeld*, what Mansfield captures in one simile. Mansfield is very good at simile; in another of her stories, 'The Voyage', a girl on a boat listens to her grandmother, lying in a bed above her saying her prayers, 'a long, soft whispering, as though someone was gently, gently rustling among tissue paper to find something'.

In New York City, the garbage collectors call maggots 'disco rice'.[57] That is as good as anything I have been discussing, and indeed there is a link between that kind of metaphor-making and Hardy's handful of fire, or Mansfield's grandmother saying her prayers like someone rummaging through tissue paper, or Marilynne Robinson's 'weedy little mortality patch'. This returns us to one of our continued questions, how the stylist manages to be a stylist without writing over his or her characters. Metaphor which is 'successful' in a poetic sense but which is at the same time character-appropriate metaphor – the kind of metaphor which this particular character or community would produce – is one way of resolving the tension between author and character, as we saw when discussing the 'leggy thing' of the nutcracker in *Pnin*. Shakespeare's fisherman likens a fish caught in a net to 'a poor man's right hanging in the law'. We might assume, by extension, that he sometimes likens the law to a fisherman's net: he finds the image which is near at hand. Chekhov describes a bird's nest as looking as if someone has left a glove in a tree – in a story about peasants. Cesare Pavese, in *The Moon and the Bonfire*, a great novel set in a poor, old-fashioned Italian village and its rural environs, describes the moon as yellow, 'like polenta'. In *Tess*, Angel and Tess are riding in a milkcart, and the milk is slopping in the pails behind them – except that Hardy says that the milk is 'clucking' in the pails, which is first of all true to life – we can instantly hear the milk *clucking* in the pails – and is also very homely and farm-like. (Likewise in the same

[57] See Elizabeth Royte, *Garbage Land: On the Secret Trail of Trash* (2005).

novel he describes a cow's udder as having teats that stick out like the short little legs on the bottom of a gypsy's cooking pot.) In *Loving*, Henry Green describes a pretty housemaid's eyes as glowing 'like plums dipped in cold water' – in a novel almost exclusively about domestic servants in a large castle. In all these cases except the Shakespearean one, metaphor is not explicitly tied to a character. It issues forth in third-person narration. So it seems to be produced by the stylish, metaphor-making author, but it also hovers around the character, and seems to emanate from that character's world.

DIALOGUE

110

In 1950, Henry Green gave a little talk on BBC radio about dialogue in fiction.[58] Green was obsessively concerned with the elimination of those vulgar spoors of presence whereby authors communicate themselves to readers: he never internalises his characters' thoughts, hardly ever explains a character's motive, and avoids the authorial adverb, which so often helpfully flags a character's emotion to readers ('She said, grandiloquently'). Green argued that dialogue is the best way to communicate with one's readers, and that nothing kills 'life' so much as 'explanation'. He imagined a husband and wife, long married, sitting at home one evening. At 9.30, the husband says that he is going across the road to the pub. Green noted that the wife's first response, 'Will you be long?', could be rendered in scores of different ways ('Back soon?' 'When will you be back?' 'Off for long?' 'How long will it be before you are back?'), each one capable of a distinct resonance of meaning. The crucial thing, maintained Green, was not to hedge the dialogue with explanation, as in:

---

[58] *Surviving: The Uncollected Writings of Henry Green*, ed. Matthew Yorke (1992).

161

'How soon d'you suppose they'll chuck you out?'

Olga, as she asked her husband this question, wore the look of a wounded animal, her lips were curled back from the teeth in a grimace and the tone of voice she used betrayed all those years a woman can give by proxy to the sawdust, the mirrors and the stale smell of beer of public bars.

Green felt strongly that such kind of authorial 'assistance' was overbearing, because in life we don't really know what people are like. 'We certainly do not know what other people are thinking and feeling. How then can the novelist be so sure?'

Green, counselling against being overbearing, is laying down a fair amount of prescription himself, and we do not need to take his doctrine scripturally. Notice that when Green does his parody of explanation, he also falls into a deliberately breathy, second-rate style ('wore the look of a wounded animal'), whereas we can imagine something more continent, less offensive: 'Olga knew what time he would come home, and in what state, stinking of beer and tobacco. Ten years of this, ten years.' Fulsome explainers like George Eliot, Henry James, Proust, Virginia Woolf, Philip Roth and many others would all have to retire themselves in Green's universe.

However, his larger argument, that dialogue should be carrying multiple meanings, and that it should mean different things to different readers at the same time, is surely right. (It can carry several indeterminate meanings for the reader *and* still be 'explained' by an author, I think, but this takes great tact.) Green offered an example of how he might proceed:

He: I think I'll go across the way now for a drink.

She: Will you be long?

He: Why don't you come too?

She: I don't think I will. Not tonight, I'm not sure, I
may.

He: Well, which is it to be?

She: I needn't say now, need I? If I feel like it I'll come
over later.

In this passage, notice that Green tries to answer one question with another, and that, very characteristically of Green's writing, the woman slides in hesitation – 'Not tonight, I'm not sure, I may.' She may be in several moods at once. As a result, the man's response, 'Well, which is it to be?' becomes harder to read, too. Is he irritated, or just mildly resigned? Does he in fact want her to come to the pub at all, or was he just saying it in the hope that she would decline? The reader tends to plump for one reading, while being aware that multiple readings are also possible; we sew ourselves into the text, becoming highly invested in *our* version of events.

There is a very good example of Green's doctrine in action in V. S. Naipaul's great novel *A House for Mr Biswas*. Mr Biswas has decided to build a house, but he only has a hundred dollars. He visits a black builder, Mr Maclean (one of the few portraits in the novel of a black Trinidadian), and gingerly poses the question. What is beautifully done is that both men are dancing a little *pas de deux* of pride and shame; each is maintaining a fiction. Mr Biswas wants Maclean to think he has enough money for a grand house; Maclean wants Biswas to think he is very busy, with lots of orders for work. And each sees through the other's fiction, of course.

163

Mr Biswas begins by suggesting that they take the thing very slowly (that way, he can pay some money each month rather than place a huge sum down immediately). Ideally, Biswas would have Maclean take about a year to build the place:

'We not bound and 'bliged to build the whole thing right away,' Mr Biswas said. 'Rome wasn't built in a day, you know.'

'So they say. But Rome get build. Anyway, as soon as I get some time I going to come and we could look at the site. You have a site?'

'Yes, yes, man. Have a site.'

'Well, in about two-three days then.'

He came early that afternoon, in hat, shoes and an ironed shirt, and they went to look at the site.

At the site, Mr Biswas announces that he wants concrete pillars, plastered and smooth. Maclean wants his cash:

'You think you could give me about a hundred and fifty dollars just to start off with?'

Mr Biswas hesitated.

'You mustn't think I want to meddle in your private affairs. I just wanting to know how much you want to spend right away.'

Mr Biswas walked away from Mr Maclean, among the bushes on the damp site, the weeds and the nettles. 'About a hundred,' he said. 'But at the end of the month I could give you a little bit more.'

'A hundred.'

'All right?'

'Yes, is all right. For a start.'

They went through the weeds and over the leaf-choked gutter to the narrow gravelly road.

'Every month we build a little,' Mr Biswas said. 'Little by little.'

'Yes, little by little.'

The dance of pride is so delicately done. Biswas first couches his shame in a classical allusion, hoping to give it a bit of grandeur ('Rome wasn't built in a day, you know'), to which Maclean replies with a practical grunt: 'So they say. But Rome get build', Naipaul subtly using Trinidadian patois – 'But Rome get build' – to separate the two men and their social status. Mr Biswas is aware of this social difference too, because, when Maclean then asks if he has a site, he tries to close the gap by also using 'black' patois: 'Yes, yes, man. Have a site.' (Whenever Biswas wants a bit of borrowed bravado, he employs the pally Caribbean word, 'man'.) Maclean affects to be so busy that he cannot come for several days, and then arrives 'early that afternoon'.

And then it all begins again, over the question of money. Maclean is perfectly aware that Mr Biswas is trying to keep face, and flatters him with the absurd 'You mustn't think I want to meddle in your private affairs.' And relentlessly, Naipaul reminds the reader that the site itself is leaf-choked and weed-infested, that the whole thing is doomed from the start. (In this, he is a good deal more of an explainer and pointer than the very reticent Henry Green.)

And the same novel reminds us that Green is not necessarily right to assume that 'dialogue is the best way for the novelist to communicate with his readers'. As much can be communicated with no speech at all. It is Christmas, and Mr Biswas, on a whim, decides to buy a hideously expensive doll's house for his daughter. He can't possibly afford it. He blows a month's wages on the gift. It is an episode of madness and bravado, of aspiration and longing and humiliation.

> He got off his bicycle and leaned it against the kerb. Before he had taken off his bicycle clips he was accosted by a heavy-lidded shopman who repeatedly sucked his teeth. The shopman offered Mr Biswas a cigarette and lit it for him. Words were exchanged. Then, with the shopman's arm around his shoulders, Mr Biswas disappeared into the shop. Not many minutes later Mr Biswas and the shopman reappeared. They were both smoking and excited. A boy came out of the shop partly hidden by the large doll's house he was carrying. The doll's house was placed on the handlebar of Mr Biswas's cycle and, with Mr Biswas on one side and the boy on the other, wheeled down the High Street.

Not a word of dialogue – indeed the opposite, the report of a dialogue we do not witness: 'Words were exchanged.' Again, this is both funny and terribly painful, because of the way Naipaul writes it up. He resolutely refuses to describe the purchase itself. Instead, he describes the scene as if the author had set up a camera outside the shop. We watch the men smoke, we watch them go in, and a few minutes later we watch them come out, 'smoking and excited'. The scene is thus like something out of the silent movies, and almost begs to be run at double speed, as farce. Passive verbs are used, precisely because Biswas is a weak, comically gentle man who thinks he is asserting himself while he is in fact generally being acted upon: 'was accosted by . . . the doll's house was placed on the handlebar . . . [was] wheeled down the High Street.' Naipaul deliberately describes this event as if Mr Biswas had nothing much to do with it, which is probably how Biswas self-forgivingly thinks of this moment. Most subtle is the decision not to represent the scene of purchase itself, the moment where money changes hands. This is the epicentre of shame for Mr Biswas, and it is as if the narrative, knowing this, *is too embarrassed to represent this shame.* Naipaul is superbly aware of this, superbly in control. He knows that the sentence 'Words were exchanged' is the pivot of the paragraph – because, of course, it is not *words* that are importantly exchanged but *money* that is crucially exchanged. And this is what cannot, must not, be described.

Several days later, the doll's house will be smashed to bits by Mr Biswas's wife, because she thinks it unfair that their daughter got such a present while none of the other children that constitute Mr Biswas's horribly extended family received anything.

TRUTH, CONVENTION, REALISM

Falsehood is so easy, truth so difficult.[59]

112

Here are two recent statements about literary realism, statements so typical of their age, so finely characteristic, so normative, that a realist novelist would have been proud to have imagined them into life. The first is by the novelist Rick Moody, writing in *Bookforum*:

> It's quaint to say so, but the realistic novel still needs a kick in the ass. The genre, with its epiphanies, its rising action, its predictable movement, its conventional humanisms, can still entertain and move us on occasion, but for me it's politically and philosophically dubious and often dull. Therefore, it needs a kick in the ass.

The second is by Patrick Giles, contributing to a long, raucous discussion about fiction, realism and fictional credibility on a literary blog called 'The Elegant Variation': 'And

---

[59] George Eliot, *Adam Bede*.

the notion that this [the realistic novel] is the supreme genre of the lit tradition is so laughable that I ain't even gonna indulge myself.'

A style unites the two statements, a down-home relaxation of diction ('kick in the ass', 'ain't even gonna'), which itself informs us about the writers' attitudes towards realism's own style: it is stuffy, correct, unprogressive, and the only way even to discuss it is to mock it with its stylistic opposite, the vernacular. Moody's three sentences efficiently compact the reigning assumptions. Realism is a 'genre' (rather than, say, a central impulse in fiction-making); it is taken to be mere dead convention, and to be related to a certain kind of traditional plot, with predictable beginnings and endings; it deals in 'round' characters, but softly and piously ('conventional humanisms'); it assumes that the world can be described, with a naively stable link between word and referent ('philosophically dubious'); and all this will tend toward a conservative or even oppressive politics ('politically and philosophically dubious').

113

This is more or less nonsense.

On the other hand, we do all know what Rick Moody means. We have all read many novels in which the machinery of convention is so rusted that nothing moves. Why, we say to ourselves, do people have to speak in quotation marks? Why do they speak in scenes of dialogue? Why so much 'conflict'? Why do people come in and out of rooms, or put down drinks, or play with their food while they are thinking of something? Why do they always have affairs? Why is there always an aged Holocaust survivor somewhere in these books? And please, whatever you do, don't introduce incest . . .

In a very witty essay written in 1935, Cyril Connolly demanded that a whole family of conventions should be butchered – 'all novels dealing with more than one generation or with any period before 1918 or with brilliant impoverished children in rectories', all novels set in Hampshire, Sussex, Oxford, Cambridge, the Essex coast, Wiltshire, Cornwall, Kensington, Chelsea, Hampstead, Hyde Park and Hammersmith.

> Many situations should be forbidden, all getting and losing of jobs, proposals of marriage, reception of love-letters by either sex . . . all allusion to illness or suicide (except insanity), all quotations, all mentions of genius, promise, writing, painting, sculpting, art, poetry, and the phrases 'I like your stuff,' 'What's his stuff like?' 'Damned good,' 'Let me make you some coffee,' all young men with ambition or young women with emotion, all remarks like 'Darling, I've found the most wonderful cottage' (flat, castle), 'Ask me any other time, dearest, only please – just this once – not now,' 'Love you – of course I love you' (don't love you) – and 'It's not that, it's only that I feel so terribly tired.'
>
> Forbidden names: Hugo, Peter, Sebastian, Adrian, Ivor, Julian, Pamela, Chloe, Enid, Inez, Miranda, Joanna, Jill, Felicity, Phyllis.
>
> Forbidden faces: all young men with curly hair or remarkable eyes, all gaunt haggard thinkers' faces, all faunlike characters, anybody over six feet, or with any distinction whatever, and all women with a nape to

their neck (he loved the way her hair curled in the little hollow at the nape of her neck).[60]

Realism, for Moody and Giles, is like Connolly's opinion of a character named Miranda or Julian; it is just another convention reflecting the aspirations of petit bourgeois readers. Barthes argued that there is no 'realistic' way to narrate the world. The nineteenth-century author's naive delusion that a word has a necessary and transparent link to its referent has been nullified. We move merely among different, competing genres of fiction-making, of which realism is just the most confused, and perhaps the most obtuse because the least self-conscious about its own procedures. Realism does not refer to reality; realism is not realistic. Realism, said Barthes, is a system of conventional codes, a grammar so ubiquitous that we do not notice the way it structures bourgeois story-telling.[61]

In practice, what Barthes means is that conventional novelists have pulled the wool over our eyes: a smooth wall of prose comes towards us, and we rather lazily gasp out loud: 'How did it all come about?' – just as Flaubert wanted us to. We no longer bother to notice such elements of fiction as the convention that people speak within quotation marks ('"Nonsense," he said, firmly'); that a character is briskly summarised in external description when he or she first enters novel or story ('She was a shortish, broad-faced woman of about fifty, with rather poorly dyed hair'); that detail is carefully chosen and helpfully 'telling' ('She noticed that his

---

[60] 'More About the Modern Novel' in *The Condemned Playground: Essays 1927–1944* (1945).
[61] See Roland Barthes, *S/Z* (1970).

171

hands shook slightly as he poured the whisky'); that dynamic and habitual detail is conflated; that dramatic action is nicely broken up by characters' reflections ('Sitting quietly at the table, his head propped on one arm, he thought again about his father'); that characters change; that stories have endings, and so on.

114

Graham Greene effortlessly produces the kind of artful-but-natural 'realism' that its opponents have in mind:

> The Professor turned away from the window. The glass was smeared, he noticed, with the faint tattoo of someone's dirty fingers. It made him think of a prisoner's hands, pushed up helplessly against the window of a van, in Beirut perhaps, or some dingy Baghdad suburb. He thought: I too am imprisoned; the mechanical teaching, the students; the weekly book reviewing, Fiona's weakness. Fiona needed him, and her need held him like an unbreaking fever.
>
> There was a knock at the door, and before the Professor could answer, Wentworth entered. There is a species of gloom unique to Friday afternoon twilight; hadn't Eliot called it 'the violet hour'? He gave Wentworth a wintry smile.
>
> 'Look old man, I'm sorry about last night.' Wentworth's high voice scratched at him like a branch against a window. He had the flat northern vowels of the grammar school scholarship boy. He had shaved inexpertly: below the smooth mineral blue of his chin,

short hairs like iron filings clustered on his pale neck.

'Forget it,' said the Professor. 'Scotch?' he offered, pouring himself a generous trench of the liquid, and dropping in two ice cubes from the sweating plastic bucket. The amber fluid looked disconcertingly like his own urine. It tasted mildly better. He thought again of Fiona, of Wentworth's shabby amorousness towards her. He had expected better of him. And Fiona's response? He could not be sure.

But that was always the way with second marriages. You had to be on your guard. The Professor was always on his guard; he had been so since the age of two, when his elder sister had stolen his favourite rosary. But who would guard the guards? God? He had believed so once; now the word 'God' was as dry in his mouth as an old communion wafer.

The Professor swilled the Scotch around his glass, making the ice cubes chatter. Wentworth, he noticed, was giving off a slight odour. It was the smell of sin.

This is a parody, but you recognise the devices. I have tied point of view to the Professor, though in a 'quiet' enough manner that the reader will hardly notice it; I have provided some telling detail; some 'good' metaphor and simile (iron filings, etc.); free indirect style ('And Fiona's response? He could not be sure. But that was always the way with second marriages'); the 'reference code', in which the author makes confident generalisations, something nineteenth-century novelists do a great deal, and which Greene is guilty of, too ('he had the flat northern vowels of the grammar school scholarship boy'); reflection ('It made him think of a prisoner's hands'), and quite a bit of tight editing and careful omission – this style being always highly reliant on what is not said, on its control of reality, its assertion of style *over* reality.

The style could be called commercial realism. It lays down a grammar of intelligent, stable, transparent story-telling, itself derived from the more original grammar of Flaubert; and of course it didn't end with Greene. Efficient contemporary realistic narrative, elegantly finished, still sounds pretty much like this. Here is John le Carré, from *Smiley's People*:

> Smiley arrived in Hamburg in mid-morning and took the airport bus to the city centre. Fog lingered and the day was very cold. In the Station Square, after repeated rejections, he found an old, thin terminus hotel with a lift licensed for three persons at a time. He signed in as Standfast, then walked as far as a car-rental agency, where he hired a small Opel which he parked in an underground garage that played softened Beethoven out of loudspeakers.

This is nice writing, for sure, and by the standards of contemporary thrillers it is magnificent (the 'thin' hotel is very good). But the detail selected is either reassuringly flat (fog, cold, the Opel car), or reassuringly 'telling': it is nothing out of the ordinary. The hotel is dabbed onto the canvas with its lift that can only carry three, the garage by its Beethoven. The selection of detail is merely the quorum necessary to convince the reader that this is 'real', that it 'really happened'. It may be 'real' but it is not *real*, because none of the details is very alive. The narrative, the grammar of the realism, exists in order to announce to us: 'This is what reality *in a novel like this* looks like – a few details that are not extraordinary

174

but nevertheless tastefully chosen and executed, enough to get the scene going.' The passage is a clever coffin of dead conventions.

115

No one would deny that writing of this sort has indeed become a kind of invisible rule-book, whereby we no longer notice its artificialities. One reason for this is economic. Commercial realism has cornered the market, has become the most powerful brand in fiction. We must expect that this brand will be economically reproduced, over and over again. That is why the complaint that realism is no more than a grammar or set of rules that obscures life is generally a better description of le Carré or P. D. James than it is of Flaubert or George Eliot or Isherwood: when a style decomposes, flattens itself down into a genre, then indeed it does become a set of mannerisms and often pretty lifeless techniques. The efficiency of the thriller genre takes just what it needs from the much less efficient Flaubert or Isherwood, and throws away what made those writers truly alive. And of course, the most economically privileged genre of this kind of largely lifeless 'realism' is commercial cinema, through which most people nowadays receive their idea of what constitutes a 'realistic' narrative.

116

Decomposition like this happens to any long-lived and successful style, surely; so the writer's – or critic's , or reader's – task is then to search for the irreducible, the superfluous, the margin of gratuity, the element in a style which cannot be easily reproduced and reduced.

117

But rather than do that, Barthes and Moody and Giles and William Gass and many other opponents of fictive convention confuse two quite different complaints. Here is Barthes in 1966: 'The function of narrative is not to "represent", it is to constitute a spectacle still very enigmatic for us but in any case not of a mimetic order ... "What takes place" in the narrative is, from the referential (reality) point of view literally nothing; "what happens" is language alone, the adventure of language, the unceasing celebration of its coming.'[62] Now, to charge fiction with conventionality is one thing; to move from this charge to the very sceptical conclusion that fictive convention can therefore never convey anything real, that narrative represents 'literally nothing', is incoherent. First, all fiction is conventional in one way or another, and if you reject a certain kind of realism for being conventional, you will also have to reject for the same reason

---

[62] From Barthes, *Image Music Text* (1966). Quoted in Antoine Compagnon, *Literature, Theory and Common Sense*, trans. Carol Cosman (2004). Notice that Barthes sounds very little different, in the end, from Plato, for whom mimesis was merely an imitation of an imitation. The real reason for the French obsession with the fraudulence of realism – and with fictional narrative in general – has to do with the existence in French of the preterite, a past tense reserved exclusively for writing about the past, and not used in speech. French fiction, in other words, has its own, dedicated language of artifice, and thus must seem, to certain minds, unbearably 'literary' and artificial.

surrealism, science fiction, self-reflexive postmodernism, novels with four different endings, and so on. Convention is everywhere, and triumphs like old age: once you have reached a certain seniority, you either die of it, or with it. One of the nice comedies of Cyril Connolly's essay is that by blacklisting every conceivable convention he effectively bans the writing of any fiction at all – 'anybody over six feet, *or with any distinction whatever*'. (My italics.) Second, just because artifice and convention are involved in a literary style does not mean that realism (or any other narrative style) is so artificial and conventional that it is incapable of referring to reality. Narrative can be conventional without being a purely *arbitrary, non-referential* technique like the form of a sonnet or the sentence with which Snoopy always begins his stories ('It was a dark and stormy night . . .')

118

Paul Valéry was hostile in a Barthes-like way to the claims of fictional narrative, and his example of an entirely arbitrary fictional premise was a sentence like: 'The Marquise went out at five o'clock.' Valéry felt, as William Gass did when discussing James's Mr Cashmore, that this sentence is exchangeable with an infinite number of other possible sentences, and that this kind of provisionality robs narrative fiction of its necessity and its claim to probability. But as soon as I place a second sentence on the page – 'That letter, received in the morning, had irritated the Marquise, and she was going to do something about it,' say – the first sentence no longer looks quite as arbitrary or peremptory or merely formal. A system of relations and affiliations is beginning to quicken. And as Julien Gracq points out,[63] 'Marquise' and 'five o'clock' are not arbitrary at all, but full of limit and suggestion: a Marquise is not an ordinary, interchangeable citizen, and five o'clock is still late afternoon while six is drinks time. So what is the Marquise going out for?

119

The point to make about convention is not that it is untruthful *per se*, but that it has a way of becoming, by repetition, steadily more and more conventional. Love becomes routine (and indeed Barthes once claimed that 'I love you' is the most clichéd thing anyone can say), but falling in love is not nullified by this fact. Metaphors become dead through overuse, but it would be insane to charge metaphor itself with deadness. When the first caveman, shivering, said that he was as cold as ice, his interlocutor probably exclaimed: 'That is pure genius!' (And after all, ice is cold.) Likewise, if someone were now to paint in the style of Rembrandt, he would be a third-rate copyist, not an original genius. These are the simplest arguments, and one should not have to make them, were it not for a persistent tendency among those hostile to verisimilitude to confuse convention with an inability to refer to anything truthful at all. Brigid Lowe[64] argues that the question of fiction's referentiality – does fiction make true statements about the world? – is the wrong one, because fiction does not ask us to *believe* things (in a philosophical sense) but to *imagine* them (in an artistic

---

[63] Julien Gracq, *En lisant en écrivant* (1980).

[64] Brigid Lowe, *Victorian Fiction and the Insights of Sympathy* (2007).

sense): 'Imagining the heat of the sun on your back is about as different an activity as can be from believing that tomorrow it will be sunny. One experience is all but sensual, the other wholly abstract. When we tell a story, although we may hope to teach a lesson, our primary objective is to produce an imaginative experience.' She proposes that we restore the Greek rhetorical term *hypotyposis*, which means to put something before our eyes, to bring it alive for us. (Somehow I don't think that *hypotyposis* will displace 'realism' as the preferred term any time soon.)

120

If we re-examine Aristotle's original formulation of mimesis, in the *Poetics*, we find that his definition is not about reference. History shows us, says Aristotle, 'what Alcibiades did'; poetry – i.e. fictional narrative – shows us 'the kind of thing that would happen' to Alcibiades. Hypothetical plausibility – probability – is the important and neglected idea, here: probability involves the defence of the credible *imagination* against the incredible. This is surely why Aristotle writes that a convincing impossibility in mimesis is always preferable to an unconvincing possibility. The burden is instantly placed not on simple verisimilitude or reference (since Aristotle concedes that an artist may represent something that is physically impossible), but on mimetic *persuasion*: it is the artist's task to convince us that this could have happened. Internal consistency and plausibility then become more important than referential rectitude. And this task will of course involve much fictive artifice and not mere reportage.

So let us replace the always problematic word 'realism' with the much more problematic word 'truth' . . . Once we throw the term 'realism' overboard, we can account for the ways in which, say, Kafka's *Metamorphosis* and Hamsun's *Hunger* and Beckett's *Endgame* are not representations of likely or typical human activity, but are nevertheless harrowingly truthful texts. This, we say to ourselves, is what it would feel like to be outcast from one's family, like an insect (Kafka), or a young madman (Hamsun), or an aged parent kept in a bin and fed pap (Beckett). There is still nothing as terrifying in contemporary fiction, not even in the blood-bin of Cormac McCarthy or the sadistic eros of Dennis Cooper, as the moment when Knut Hamsun's narrator, in *Hunger*, a starving young intellectual, puts his finger in his mouth and starts eating himself. None of us, I hope, has done this, or will ever want to. But Hamsun has made us share it, has made us feel it. Dr Johnson, in his 'Preface to Shakespeare', reminds us that 'imitations produce pain or pleasure, not because they are mistaken for realities, but because they bring realities to mind.'

121

Convention itself, like metaphor itself, is not dead; but it is always dying. So the artist is always trying to outwit it. But in outwitting it, the artist is always establishing another dying convention. It is this paradox that explains the further, well-known literary-historical paradox, namely that poets and novelists repeatedly attack one kind of realism only to argue for their own kind of realism. (In Barthes's or William Gass's sceptical universe, in which narrative is not mimetic at all, this ought to make no sense.) It is summarised in Flaubert's remark about pornography: 'Obscene books are immoral because untruthful. When reading them, one says, "That's not the way things are." Mind you, I detest realism, though I am claimed as one of its pontiffs.' On the one hand, Flaubert wants nothing to do with the movement of 'realism'; on the other, he deems certain books 'untruthful' because they do not depict things as they are. (Chekhov used a similar formulation when watching an Ibsen play: 'But Ibsen is no playwright . . . Ibsen just doesn't know life. In life it simply isn't like that.') Thomas Hardy argued that art wasn't realistic because art is 'a disproportioning – (i.e. distorting, throwing out of proportion) – of realities, to show more clearly the features that matter in those realities, which, if merely copied or reported inventorially, might possibly be observed, but would more probably be overlooked. Hence "realism" is not art.' Yet Hardy, of course, no less than Flaubert, strove to write novels and poems that show 'the way things are'. Who has written more beautifully or more truthfully than Hardy about rural communities, or about grief?

These writers rejected mere photographic fidelity, because art selects and shapes. But they revered truth and truthfulness. They believed, as George Eliot put it in her essay 'The Natural History of German Life', that 'Art is the nearest thing to life; it is a mode of amplifying experience and extending our contact with our fellowman beyond the bounds of our personal lot.' The great Victorian realist is being precise here: art is not life itself, art is always an artifice, is always mimesis – but art is the *nearest thing* to life. Yet Eliot begins her novel *Adam Bede*:

With a single drop of ink for a mirror, the Egyptian sorcerer undertakes to reveal to any chance comer far-reaching visions of the past. This is what I undertake to do for you, reader. With this drop of ink at the end of my pen I will show you the roomy workshop of Mr Jonathan Burge, carpenter and builder in the village of Hayslope, as it appeared on the eighteenth of June, in the year of our Lord 1799.

The novelist shows you life as it is; but she is also an Egyptian sorcerer, happy to admit that she is conjuring it from nothing in front of you (i.e. *hypotyposis*). Most major movements in literature in the last two centuries have invoked a desire to capture the 'truth' of 'life' (or 'the way things are'), even as the definition of what is 'realistic' changes. (And of course even as what counts as 'life' changes somewhat too – but that *this* definition changes does not mean that there is no such thing as life.) Woolf rightly complained that E. M. Forster, in *Aspects of the Novel*, was always invoking 'life', and that it reflected a residual hearty Victorianism on Forster's part. Woolf properly argued that we judge fiction's success not just for its ability to evoke 'life' but for its ability to delight us with more formal properties, like pattern and language:

> At this point perhaps the pertinacious pupil will demand: but what is this 'life' that keeps on cropping up so mysteriously in books about fiction? Why is it absent in a pattern and present in a tea party? Why, if we get a keen and genuine pleasure from the pattern in the *Golden Bowl*, is it less valuable than the emotion which Trollope gives us when he describes a lady

drinking tea in a parsonage? Surely the definition of life is too arbitrary and requires to be expanded? Why, again, should the final test of plot, character, story and the other ingredients of a novel lie in their power to imitate life? Why should a real chair be better than an imaginary elephant?[65]

But on the other hand, she also complained that 'life escapes' from the fiction of Arnold Bennett and his Edwardian generation, and that 'perhaps without life nothing else is worth while'.[66] She praised Joyce for coming closer to 'life', and sweeping away a host of dead conventions. Alain Robbe-Grillet, in his book *Pour un nouveau roman*, rightly says that 'All writers believe they are realists. None ever calls himself abstract, illusionistic, chimerical, fantastic.' But, he goes on to say, if all these writers are mustered under the same flag, it is not because they agree about what realism is; it is because they want to use their different idea of realism to tear each other apart.

If we add to these examples the invocations of 'Nature' beloved of neoclassical critics, the overwhelmingly strong Aristotelian tradition with its distinction between probability and the improbably marvellous (accepted by Cervantes, Fielding, Richardson, Dr Johnson), the claim made by Wordsworth and Coleridge that the poems in *Lyrical Ballads* offer 'a natural delineation of human passions, human characters, and human incidents', and so on, we are likely to think of the desire to be truthful about life – the desire to produce art that accurately sees 'the way things are' – as a

---

[65] Virginia Woolf, 'Is Fiction An Art?' (1927).
[66] Virginia Woolf, 'Modern Fiction' (1922).

universal literary motive and project, the broad central language of the novel and drama: what James in *What Maisie Knew* calls 'the firm ground of fiction, through which indeed there curled the blue river of truth'. 'Realism' and the technical or philosophical squabbles it has engendered seem like a school of bright red herrings.

122

And in our own reading lives, every day, we come across that blue river of truth, curling somewhere; we encounter scenes and moments and perfectly placed words in fiction and poetry, in film and drama, which strike us with their truth, which move and sustain us, which shake habit's house to its foundations: King Lear asking forgiveness of Cordelia; Lady Macbeth hissing at her husband during the banquet; Pierre almost executed by French soldiers in *War and Peace*; the tattered band of survivors wandering the streets of an unnamed city in Saramago's *Blindness*; Dorothea Brooke in Rome, realising that she has married a man whose soul is dead; Gregor Samsa, being pushed back into his room by his own, horrified father; Kirilov, in *The Possessed*, writing his suicide note, with the awful Peter Verkhovensky by his side, suddenly and ridiculously bursting out: 'Wait! I want to draw a face with the tongue out on the top . . . I want to tell them off!' Or the beautiful little scene in *Persuasion* when Anne Elliot, kneeling on the floor, and keen to get a heavy two-year-old boy off her back, is suddenly relieved of the burden by the man she secretly loves, Captain Wentworth:

Someone was taking him from her, though he had bent down her head so much, that his little sturdy hands were unfastened from around her neck, and he was resolutely borne away, before she knew that Captain Wentworth had done it.

Her sensations on the discovery made her perfectly speechless. She could not even thank him. She could only hang over little Charles, with most disordered feelings.

Or the last chapter of Willa Cather's *Death Comes for the Archbishop*, some of the most exquisite pages ever written in American fiction.[67] Father Latour has returned to die in Santa Fe, near his cathedral: 'In New Mexico he always awoke a young man; not until he rose and began to shave did he realise that he was growing older. His first consciousness was a sense of the light dry wind blowing in through the windows, with the fragrance of hot sun and sage-brush and sweet clover; a wind that made one's body feel light and one's heart cry "To-day, to-day," like a child's.' Lying in his bed, he thinks about his old life in France, about his new life in the New World, about the architect, Molny, who built his Romanesque cathedral in Santa Fe, and about death. He is lucid and calm:

He observed also that there was no longer any perspective in his memories. He remembered his winters with his cousins on the Mediterranean when he was a little boy, his student days in the Holy City, as clearly as he

---

[67] Pages surely influenced by Chekhov's story about a dying bishop, 'The Bishop', and an influence, in turn, on Marilynne Robinson's *Gilead*.

remembered the arrival of M. Molny and the building of his Cathedral. He was soon to have done with calendared time, and it had already ceased to count for him. He sat in the middle of his own consciousness; none of his former states of mind were lost or outgrown. They were all within reach of his hand, and all comprehensible.

Sometimes, when Magdalena or Bernard came in and asked him a question, it took him several seconds to bring himself back to the present. He could see they thought his mind was failing; but it was only extraordinarily active in some other part of the great picture of his life – some part of which they knew nothing.

123

Realism, seen broadly as truthfulness to the way things are, cannot be mere verisimilitude, cannot be mere lifelikeness, or lifesameness, but what I must call *lifeness*: life on the page, life brought to different life by the highest artistry. And it cannot be a genre; instead, it makes other forms of fiction seem like genres. For realism of this kind – lifeness – is the origin. It teaches everyone else; it schools its own truants: it is what allows magical realism, hysterical realism, fantasy, science fiction, even thrillers, to exist. It is nothing like as naive as its opponents charge; almost all the great twentieth-century realist novels also reflect on their own making, and are full of artifice. All the greatest realists, from Austen to Alice Munro, are at the same time great formalists. But this will be unceasingly difficult: for the writer has to act as if the available novelistic methods are continually about to turn into mere convention and so has to try to outwit that inevitable ageing. The true writer, that free servant of life, is one who must always be acting as if life were a category beyond anything the novel had yet grasped; as if life itself were always on the verge of becoming conventional.

BIBLIOGRAPHY

Novels, short stories, and narratives referred to or quoted from in this book are listed below. In the interest of evoking a sense of historical passage and context, I have ordered them by first date of publication in their original language. Translators have been credited in those cases in which I have quoted at any length from one particular translation.

Miguel de Cervantes, *Don Quixote* (1605 and 1615)

The Bible, King James Version (1611)

Daniel Defoe, *Robinson Crusoe* (1719)

Henry Fielding, *Joseph Andrews* (1742), *Tom Jones* (1749)

Denis Diderot, *Rameau's Nephew* (written in the 1760s, published in 1784)

Jane Austen, *Pride and Prejudice* (1813), *Emma* (1816), *Persuasion* (1818)

Stendhal, *The Red and the Black* (1830)

A. S. Pushkin, *Eugene Onegin* (1823–31)

Honore de Balzac, *La peau de chagrin* (1831), *Splendeurs et misères des courtisanes* (1839–47)

Stendhal, *The Charterhouse of Parma* (1839)

Charlotte Brontë, *Jane Eyre* (1847)

W. M. Thackeray, *Vanity Fair* (1848)

Charles Dickens, *David Copperfield* (1850)

Gustave Flaubert, *Madame Bovary* (1857, trans. G. Wall)

George Eliot, *Adam Bede* (1859)

Charles Dickens, *Great Expectations* (1861)

F. M. Dostoevsky, *Notes From Underground* (1864), *Crime and Punishment* (1866)

Gustave Flaubert, *Sentimental Education* (1869, trans. Robert Baldick)

L. N. Tolstoy, *War and Peace*, (1869, trans. Louise and Aylmer Maude)

George Eliot, *Middlemarch* (1872)

Thomas Hardy, *Far from the Madding Crowd* (1874)

L. N. Tolstoy, *Anna Karenina* (1877)

F. M. Dostoevsky, *The Brothers Karamazov* (1880)

Henry James, *The Portrait of a Lady* (1881)

L. N. Tolstoy, *The Death of Ivan Ilyich* (1886)

Thomas Hardy, *The Mayor of Casterbridge* (1886)

Guy de Maupassant, *Pierre and Jean* (1888)

Knut Hamsun, *Hunger* (1890)

Thomas Hardy, *Tess* (1891)

A. P. Chekhov, 'Ward No. 6' (1892), 'Rothschild's Fiddle' (1894)

Theodor Fontane, *Effi Briest* (1894)

Stephen Crane, *The Red Badge of Courage* (1895)

Henry James, *What Maisie Knew* (1897)

A. P. Chekhov, 'The Lady with the Little Dog' (1899)

Theodore Dreiser, *Sister Carrie* (1900)

Thomas Mann, *Buddenbrooks* (1901)

A. P. Chekhov, 'The Bishop' (1902)

Joseph Conrad, *Heart of Darkness* (1902)

Beatrix Potter, *The Tailor of Gloucester* (1903)

Rainer Maria Rilke, *The Notebooks of Malte Laurids Brigge* (1910)

L. N. Tolstoy, *Hadji Murad* (1912)
Marcel Proust, *Remembrance of Things Past* (1913–27, trans.
   C. K. Scott Moncrieff and Terence Kilmartin)
James Joyce, *Dubliners* (1914)
Franz Kafka, *Metamorphosis* (1915)
D. H. Lawrence, *The Rainbow* (1915)
James Joyce, *A Portrait of the Artist as a Young Man* (1916)
D. H. Lawrence, *Sea and Sardinia* (1921)
Katherine Mansfield, *The Garden Party and Other Stories* (1922)
James Joyce, *Ulysses* (1922)
Sinclair Lewis, *Babbitt* (1922)
Italo Svevo, *Confessions of Zeno* (1923)
Thomas Mann, *The Magic Mountain* (1924)
Virginia Woolf, *To the Lighthouse* (1927)
Willa Cather, *Death Comes for the Archbishop* (1927)
William Faulkner, *As I Lay Dying* (1930)
Virginia Woolf, *The Waves* (1931)
Joseph Roth, *The Radetzky March* (1932)
Louis-Ferdinand Céline, *Journey to the End of the Night* (1932)
Christopher Isherwood, *Goodbye to Berlin* (1939)
Robert McLoskey, *Make Way for Ducklings* (1941)
Henry Green, *Caught* (1943)
Henry Green, *Loving* (1945)
Evelyn Waugh, *Brideshead Revisited* (1945)
Vladimir Nabokov, 'First Love' (1948)
Cesare Pavese, *The Moon and the Bonfire* (1950)
Ralph Ellison, *Invisible Man* (1952)
Vladimir Nabokov, *Lolita* (1955)
Saul Bellow, *Seize the Day* (1956)
Vladimir Nabokov, *Pnin* (1957)
V. S. Naipaul, *A House for Mr Biswas* (1961)
Muriel Spark, *The Prime of Miss Jean Brodie* (1961)

John Updike, *Of the Farm* (1965)
Thomas Pynchon, *The Crying of Lot 49* (1966)
Frederick Exley, *A Fan's Notes* (1968)
B. S. Johnson, *Christie Malry's Own Double Entry* (1973)
John le Carré, *Smiley's People* (1979)
Thomas Bernhard, *Wittgenstein's Nephew* (1982)
José Saramago, *The Year of the Death of Ricardo Reis* (1984)
Cormac McCarthy, *Blood Meridian* (1985)
Philip Roth, *The Counterlife* (1986)
Kazuo Ishiguro, *The Remains of the Day* (1989)
Norman Rush, *Mating* (1991)
W. G. Sebald, *The Emigrants* (1992)
Cormac McCarthy, *All the Pretty Horses* (1992)
Philip Roth, *Sabbath's Theater* (1995)
Roberto Bolaño, *The Savage Detectives* (1998)
Ian McEwan, *Atonement* (2001)
Norman Rush, *Mortals* (2003)
David Foster Wallace, *Oblivion and other stories* (2004)
Marilynne Robinson, *Gilead* (2004)
J. M. Coetzee, *Elizabeth Costello* (2004)
Thomas Pynchon, *Against the Day* (2006)
John Updike, *Terrorist* (2006)

INDEX

Naipaul, V. S., 127; *A House for Mr Biswas*,
    18–19, 163–7
Nietzsche, Friedrich, 120, 123; *Beyond Good
    and Evil*, 137
Nixon, Richard, 51–2
Nuttall, A. D.; *A New Mimesis*, 66

O'Faolain, Sean, 143
Orwell, George; 'A Hanging', 67
O'Toole, Peter, 79

Pavese, Cesare, 20; *The Moon and the Bonfire*,
    159
Paz, Octavio; *The Labyrinth of Solitude*, 128
Pessoa, Fernando, 85–6
Plato, 130, 176
Poe, Edgar Allan, 128
Pope, Alexander, 59, *The Rape of The Lock*, 17
Powers, J. F., 143
Pritchett, V. S., 'The Wheelbarrow', 104
Proust, Marcel, 100, 146, 162; *À la recherche
    du temps perdu*, 49, 123–5; *Contre Sainte-
    Beuve*, 39
Pushkin, Alexander; *Eugene Onegin*, 55, 84
Pynchon, Thomas; *Against The Day*, 115; *The
    Crying of Lot 49*, 27; *Gravity's Rainbow*,
    115

Rameau, Jean-Philippe, 116–7
Rilke, Rainer Maria; *The Notebooks of Malte
    Laurids Brigge*, 39–40, 61
Robbe-Grillet, Alain, 91, 142; *Pour un nouveau
    roman*, 183
Robinson, Marilynne; *Gilead*, 138–9, 185;
    Housekeeping, 139
Roth, Joseph; *The Emperor's Tomb*, 124; *The
    Radetzky March*, 71, 153
Roth, Philip, 145, 149, 162; *The Counterlife*,
    92–4; *Sabbath's Theater*, 150–2
Rousseau, Jean Jacques; *The Confessions*, 124
Rulfo, Juan; *Pedro Páramo*, 128
Rush, Norman; *Mating*, 150; *Mortals*, 156–7
Ruskin, John, 1, 2, 139

Salerno-Sonnenberg, Nadja, 72
Saramago, José; *Blindness*, 184; *The Year of the
    Death of Ricardo Reis*, 85–7
Sarraute, Nathalie, 142
Scott, Sir Walter, 116
Scotus, Duns, 54
Sebald, W. G., 5–6, 93–4; *The Emigrants*, 100
Seinfeld, 158
Shaftesbury, Earl of, 130

Shakespeare, William, 94, 107; *Hamlet*, 100;
    Henry IV Part I, 55, 154; *Henry V*, 102–4;
    King Lear, 25; *Macbeth*, 108–13, 154;
    Pericles, 154, 159
Shklovsky, Viktor, 1–2; *Theory of Prose*, 22,
    114
Simpson, Joe, 48
Smith, Adam; *Lectures of Rhetoric and Belles
    Lettres*, 58, 114; *The Theory of Moral
    Sentiments*, 130
Smith, Zadie, 105
Spark, Muriel, 105, 127; *The Prime of Miss
    Jean Brodie*, 87–93, 149–50
Stendhal: (Beyle, Marie Henri), 63; *The
    Charterhouse of Parma*, 52; *The Red and the
    Black*, 52, 117–9
Svevo, Italo, 5, 7; *Confessions of Zeno*, 84

Thackeray, William Makepeace, 104; *Vanity
    Fair*, 89, 99–100
Theophrastus, 114–5
Tolstoy, Leo, 5, 22, 94, 101, 146; *Anna
    Karenina*, 51–2, 71; *The Death of Ivan
    Ilyich*, 8, 55; *Hadji Murad*, 133; *War and
    Peace*, 49, 67, 89, 130–31, 135–6, 184
Trollope, Anthony, 94
Turgenev, Ivan, 63, 142
Twain, Mark, 138

Updike, John, 147; *Of the Farm*, 62; *Terrorist*,
    23, 28, 42, 70

Valéry, Paul, 177–80
Verga, Giovanni, 20, 27

Wallace, David Foster, 25–8, 147, 150; 'The
    Suffering Channel', 26
Waugh, Evelyn, 104, 116
Wells, H. G., 104
Wharton, Edith, 77
Williams, Bernard, 100, 133–5
Wilson, Angus, 105
Wilson, Edmund, 63, 156
Wittgenstein, Ludwig; *Culture and Value*, 154
Wodehouse, P.G., 7
Woolf, Leonard, 96
Woolf, Virginia, 50, 93–4, 116, 125–6, 139,
    182–3; *To the Lighthouse*, 135, 158; *The
    Waves*, 140
Wordsworth, William, 183; *The Prelude*, 40–41
Worthen, John, 57

Yeats, W. B., 18, 152